Managing Emotions in Organizations

"It is something of a mystery as to why and how some international acquisitions succeed, and others fail to achieve their expected performance. Negative emotions in the workforce are suspected of playing an important role, but whether these are consequences or causes of underperformance remains obscure. This in depth case study research by Dr. Riikka Harikkala-Laihinen gives us some pointers that, for many of us, will chime with our experience. International acquisitions typically cut across cultural boundaries, but it is not these boundaries themselves that are the problem. It is the way that we, and management respond to them, to anticipate concerns. This is important because, it puts the ball back firmly in the court of management, and gives agency to the firm's leadership. Dr. Harikkala-Laihinen's analysis suggests that the key is positivity. This is not merely spin. Conviction by leaders, and action through, for example, training to engender inclusivity and positive emotional attitudes allays the natural fears of staff that eat away at their ability to work together across cultures and perform at their best. This individual and team level underperformance adds up to, not surprisingly, underperformance at the acquisition level. But, positivity, it is suggested, can turn outcomes around. This research is important both for the academic subject field of International Business, as it gets to the heart of questions that remain with us today, and are still unresolved. It is important for international management practice, precisely because it suggests something can be done, and that where there is a will, there is always a way. That, quite simply, is the power of positivity."

—Jeremy Clegg, *Jean Monnet Professor of European Integration & International Business Management, University of Leeds*

"It is often taken for granted that business decisions, especially those involved in mergers and acquisitions are always coldly calculated and rational. In this book, Dr. Harikkala-Laihinen demonstrates that nothing could be further from the truth. In three meticulously researched case studies involving Finnish and German companies, she lays bare the intensely emotional nature of decision-making at all stages of the merger process. As such, the book should be a must-read for business managers seeking to enhance their business though engaging in mergers or acquisitions."

—Neal M. Ashkanasy, *Professor of Management, University of Queensland*

"This book highlights that companies are not just numbers and machines but consist of human beings. The combination of theoretical research with practical case studies gives valuable insight of the importance of recognizing emotions and proactive leadership especially in times of change. Particularly in M&A activities, starting with the why, communicating actively and engaging employees can smoothen the path on the change journey. This book offers excellent points for reflection and gives valuable ideas of do's and don'ts for leaders involved in M&A and organizational change initiatives."

—Henri Hilke, *Vice President, Human Resources, ABB Oy*

Riikka Harikkala-Laihinen

Managing Emotions in Organizations

Positive Employee Experiences Following Acquisitions

palgrave
macmillan

Riikka Harikkala-Laihinen
Turku School of Economics
University of Turku
Turku, Finland

ISBN 978-3-030-60566-7 ISBN 978-3-030-60567-4 (eBook)
https://doi.org/10.1007/978-3-030-60567-4

This Palgrave Macmillan imprint is published by the registered company Springer Nature Switzerland AG.
The registered company address is: Gewerbestrasse 11, 6330 Cham, Switzerland

Acknowledgments

Turning the idea of managing emotions in organizations in a positive way into a book has been a rollercoaster of ideas, setbacks and hard work. I wish to offer particular thanks to Professor Niina Nummela and Postdoctoral Researcher Johanna Raitis from the University of Turku and Lecturer Melanie Hassett from the Sheffield University Management School for your cooperation in collecting and analyzing the data for Chap. 2. Your insight and support was invaluable in finishing this work.

I also want to thank Professor Jeremy Clegg from the University of Leeds, Professor Neal Ashkanasy from the University of Queensland and Vice President of Human Resources Henri Hilke from ABB for the time and effort they have taken to write endorsements for my book. Along with the editorial team at Palgrave, I want to especially thank the anonymous editor from Scribendi for the years of excellent cooperation. Your attention to detail not only in grammatical but also content matters is beyond comparison.

The research process for this book was partially supported by Tekes—The Finnish Funding Agency for Technology and Innovation, the Marcus Wallenberg Economic Research Foundation and the University of Turku Foundation.

Acknowledgements

Contents

List of Figures

List of Tables

CHAPTER 1

Introduction

Abstract This chapter provides a detailed overview of the relevant concepts and theories that this book builds on. The increasing interest in the soft side of business has been found to have influenced the emergence of emotion research in organizations. Based on cognitive appraisal theory, emotions are short-term reactions to events in our surroundings that we believe to be personally relevant. At work, affective events theory suggests such emotions arise from interpersonal or task-related incidents and that they modify behaviour. Change periods, such as post-acquisition integration, are very likely to trigger emotions. However, whereas previous acquisition research has focused on negative emotional states, this book builds on emerging discoveries of how positive emotions can ease change.

Keywords Cognitive appraisal theory • Affective events theory • Post-acquisition integration

1 Setting the Scene

In writing this book, I ask where the place for humanity is in the bottom line of a company. We have a tendency to reduce business to numbers, considering returns on investments, profit and loss statements, operating margins and so forth. Yet, we forget that behind each number is a living breathing human being: CEOs who draw strategic outlines, salesclerks

R. Harikkala-Laihinen, *Managing Emotions in Organizations*,
https://doi.org/10.1007/978-3-030-60567-4_1

handling orders and billing, line workers twisting bolts. These people do not stop being human as they enter the workplace. They do not stop experiencing emotions, they do not become perfectly rational and predictable and, often, they do not enjoy being considered as a mere number on the company's fact sheet. But why should this matter?

In the past few decades, the soft side of business has gained increasing attention. Although buzzwords such as efficiency and costs continue to intrigue scholars and practitioners alike, the rising levels of distrust and dissatisfaction among employees have driven attention towards the more human aspects of business (Karlgaard 2014). Thanks to scholarly attention, we now know that emotions pervade not just our everyday behaviour, but also organizations (Ashkanasy 2003).

The shift in attention towards the softer side of business has been very influential in the field of mergers and acquisitions (M&As). The human side of acquisitions used to be considered through ticking a box; in effect, considering human resource (HR) management in an acquisition checklist, entailing everything from salaries to corporate culture. Yet, in the modern world, it is becoming increasingly clear that the value of a company cannot be measured solely through traditional tangible assets. Instead, the value of a company may largely reside in its employees (Wilkinson and Pickett 2010).

Indeed, the past 30 years have shown increasing attention being placed on the human side of acquisitions (e.g. Sarala et al. 2019), deepening our understanding of post-acquisition integration as a softer human process in addition to the hard cold facts (Cartwright and Cooper 1995). The hard and the soft have been found to be complementary; whereas task integration focuses on realizing operational synergies, human integration aims at creating positive attitudes and unification (Birkinshaw et al. 2000). Stemming from this discovery, a growing body of literature argues that acquisition failure is often caused by sociocultural challenges during the integration (e.g. Datta 1991; Marks and Mirvis 2011; Raitis et al. 2018).

At the same time, acquisition scholars have become increasingly interested in emotions, studying them from various perspectives, including coping, antecedents of negative emotions, emotional outcomes, emotional attending, emotion regulation, employee behaviour and managerial reactions (Fugate et al. 2002; Kiefer 2005; Clarke and Salleh 2011; Reus 2012; Fink and Yolles 2015; Gunkel et al. 2015; Durand 2016). The consensus seems to be that during acquisitions, emotions are usually triggered by perceived challenges in upholding accustomed organizational values, and that they normally peak around a public announcement (Sinkovics et al. 2011). Yet, despite empirical evidence regarding positive emotions (e.g. Kusstatscher 2006; Raitis et al. 2017), previous research seems to conclude that emotions are typically negative and cause poor organizational outcomes (Graebner et al. 2017). Thus, a more positive perspective on sociocultural integration seems warranted (Stahl et al. 2013). However, first it is necessary to understand exactly what emotions are.

2 What Is Emotion?

2.1 Emotion, Affect and Mood

Historically, emotions have been considered primitive—as something undesirable, unintelligent and unreliable—and which should be restrained by logic (Solomon 2008). These sentiments, however, began to fade in the mid-twentieth century, with emotions becoming a central phenomenon in research around the new millennium (Ben-Ze'ev and Krebs 2018). While emotions can still be considered currents in the ocean, flashes of unwitting primal passion, pushing us to behave in certain ways, we can always identify their object: Emotions are fundamentally about something (Nussbaum 2004). This separates emotions from other affective phenomena.

Affect refers to a myriad of phenomena, such as emotion or mood (Guerrero et al. 1996). A core affect reflects a state that can be positioned along two separate continuums: pleasure/displeasure and activation/deactivation. It directs our attention towards similarly valenced states and motivates behaviour. When the core affect is prolonged but not directed at an object, it becomes a mood (Russell 2003). *Moods* reflect an attitude towards our environment, without a definable cause (Guerrero et al. 1996). Only when the affective state has a cause—a trigger—does it become an emotion.

Emotion is a generic label through which we describe experiences (Gordon 1987). While many definitions have arisen, modern research seems to agree that emotions are componential; they include appraisal, action readiness, physiological cues, subjective feelings and behavioural outcomes (Scherer and Moors 2019). This book takes a subjective experiential viewpoint on emotion that emphasizes cognition and appraisal (cf. Kleinginna and Kleinginna 1981).

2.2 Cognitive Appraisal Theory

The mother of *cognitive appraisal theory* (see Cornelius 2006), Magda Arnold (1960), claimed that to become emotional, events must be assessed against previous experience. In other words, emotion requires perception and appraisal. Thus, emotions are reactions. They are elicited in the external environment, appraised based on previous knowledge, differentiated through their influence on activation, physiological responses and motor expressions, and finally, they are represented through a subjective feeling and categorized label (Scherer and Moors 2019). In this process, motivation and cognition are central. Cognitive mediation and evaluation allows an individual to tap into inner ideas of importance or unimportance, thereby determining whether an event is likely damaging or favourable (Lazarus 1991).

The key element of appraisal reflects a degree of personal relevance in emotion elicitation; an evaluation of how important a specific situation is to the self. Perceiving a situation or event as relevant to personal well-being is a prerequisite of the said situation becoming emotional (Lazarus 1991). This highlights the notion that, fundamentally, emotions are judgements (Solomon 2003). The reactive, judgement-based viewpoint of emotion implies that emotions are of short duration. Emotions are episodes that include a trigger, an appraisal of the trigger and a subsequent appraisal-congruent reaction (Fredrickson 2001). Moreover, triggered emotions activate individuals' motivational goals, thereby modifying behaviour (Wang et al. 2018). Thus, emotions encompass both psychological and physiological components (Izard 1972; cf. Cabanac 2002; Scherer 2005; Ekman and Cordaro 2011). The psychological aspects include cognitive processing (i.e. appraisal) and subjective experience (i.e. felt emotion), whereas the physiological aspects are visible in bodily changes (e.g. a change in heart rate) and motor expression (e.g. smiling) (Scherer 2005). As a consequence, emotions can influence behaviour, such as drawing away from an event that is evaluated as frightening (Izard 1972; Scherer 2005).

Nevertheless, emotions often appear to be reflexive. Indeed, some emotions can be considered evolutionary neurobiological substrates. Such basic emotions are automatic non-conscious responses to external stimuli. In contrast, emotion schemas are more complex processes where learned associations differentiate emotion labels (Izard 2007). Despite their responsive nature, emotions are not always sequential. Instead, they may overlap. Individuals are able to experience several, even conflicting emotions at any one time (Carrera and Oceja 2009). So, what makes emotions positive or negative?

2.3 Defining Positive and Negative

The positive or negative classification of emotions is based on their perceived hedonic quality—whether they feel good or feel bad (Gordon 1987). The pleasure/displeasure and activation/deactivation continuums mean that positive and negative need not be opposites. Instead, they are independent and uncorrelated; both positive (pleasure) and negative (displeasure) affect can have a high or low state of arousal (Watson and Tellegen 1985). Thus, the concepts of positive pleasure and negative displeasure are considered more bipolar in nature and exist independently of each other (Russell and Carroll 1999). If we consider the two continuums as a circumplex, movement towards the centre reflects lower arousal, whereas movement towards the outer rim signals an intensified effect. Thus, highly positive affect finds its opposite in a low positive state. For example, excitement can be considered as the opposite of dullness. Conversely, fear (high negative) can be considered as the opposite of relaxation (low negative) (Watson and Tellegen 1985).

Apart from the nature of emotions, the characteristics of the experiencing individual influence the perception of an emotion as positive or negative. For example, an event may be considered pleasant or unpleasant based on personal traits or cultural background (cf. Bowen 2014). Thus, positive refers to personal sensations of pleasure and goal-congruency, whereas negative refers to personal sensations of displeasure and goal incongruence. Often, positive emotions seem more attractive than negative ones. Nevertheless, individuals can take pleasure in negative emotions (e.g. enjoying sadness) or they can feel bad about experiencing positive ones (e.g. being ashamed of feeling pride). Thus, one's personal attitude or anticipation of an emotion also influences the experience (Gordon 1987). In fact, emotions are organismic. Emotions represent the complex evaluation of individuals' physical and mental well-being in relation to their personal life goals (Lazarus 1991). Considering the activating element through behavioural outcomes adds to this complexity. For example, anger and fear are both negative emotions, yet anger is likely to aggravate, whereas fear is likely to lead to disengaging (Ashkanasy and Dorris 2017).

3 Emotions in the Workplace

3.1 Emotions in Organizations

At work, emotions appear across five organizational levels. First, at the within-person level, individuals experience temporal emotions triggered by daily work events. Second, at the between-persons level, employees' dispositional tendencies come into play, shaping how emotions emerge and influence organizations. Third, at the interpersonal interaction level, employees perceive others' emotion expressions, giving way to emotional communication. Fourth, at the group level, employees seek cohesion, triggering emotional convergence and enabling the generation of collective values. Finally, at the organizational level, the organizational culture and climate create the basis for collective emotional states to emerge (Ashkanasy 2003; Ashkanasy and Dorris 2017).

Collective emotional states are often called group emotions. Although emotions are subjective by nature, when a number of individuals simultaneously experience a similar emotion in response to the same event, the emergent collective state is referred to as a group emotion (Kemper 2002). Group emotions usually arise based on membership in a particular social group, because members are more likely to have similar reactions to events that are perceived as relevant to the particular group (Goldenberg et al. 2014). Such membership gives rise to group-based emotions: experiences born from groups, such as national pride. Emotions can also be born in groups and thus become group-shared, such as collective excitement at a rock concert (Menges and Kilduff 2015). At work, group-based emotions likely stem from organizational identity, whereas group-shared emotions reflect reactions to everyday occurrences (Harikkala-Laihinen 2019).

Change is a key emotion trigger at work. Emotions allow employees to construct meaning during change periods, influencing adaptation and enabling the individual to connect with the social surroundings (Kiefer 2002). Change can trigger both positive and negative emotions, and can be either activating or deactivating in terms of employee involvement. Change acceptance is an inactive positive reaction born out of calmness or relaxation. Change disengagement is similarly inactive, but on the negative side. Disengagement is triggered by experiences such as sadness, helplessness or despair. The active negative change resistance in turn occurs when employees become distinctly angry or stressed. The ideal state, positive and activating change proactivity, is linked to experiences of excitement and enthusiasm (Oreg et al. 2018). During change periods, employees' behavioural responses are directly linked to the emotional reactions triggered by events at work (Smollan 2006).

3.2 Affective Events Theory

Affective events theory is a perspective on emotion in organizations (Weiss and Beal 2005). It explains emotion elicitation in the workplace, drawing a line between the somewhat stable work environment and dynamic events within that environment as emotion triggers. Affective events theory posits that events within the workplace are directly linked to work-related behaviour and attitudes (Weiss and Cropanzano 1996). An event in the affective events theory refers to a discrete episode, an incident bound in space and time, with a clear beginning and end. To become a noteworthy event, the incident must carry an air of discontinuity that separates it from the organization's routines (Morgeson et al. 2015).

What makes the event affective is that it stimulates a reaction based on a job-related agent, object, or occurrence. This reaction includes appraisal and an emotional reaction, and can reflect either a transitory or ongoing work-related goal (Basch and Fisher 1998). The affective events can be categorized as being in the task-related or interpersonal spheres. Task-related events influence the execution of job assignments, whereas interpersonal events concern colleagues (Casper et al. 2019). In addition to the triggering event itself, the work environment may influence the resulting emotional reaction. For example, should the atmosphere at work be stressful, a superior's critique is likely to cause anger, which leads to job dissatisfaction and possibly even an open argument or leaving the company (Mignonac and Herrbach 2004). Nevertheless, individuals differ in their personal disposition towards emotions, often highlighting either positive or negative experiences, thus also influencing which emotions are likely to emerge at work (Fisher 2002).

3.3 Emotions Following Acquisitions

Focusing on the human side of acquisitions reveals them to be a process of adaptation (Cartwright and Cooper 1995). This process is often named acculturation; the making of a unified culture from previously separate beliefs, assumptions and values (Larsson and Lubatkin 2001). Acculturation includes the coming together, clashing and adaptation necessary to achieve a harmonious coexistence (Nahavandi and Malekzadeh 1988; Rottig et al. 2013). The resultant conflict and adaptation often lead to change resistance, at worst giving rise to the merger syndrome—a fear-the-worst response increasing stress and anxiety (Marks and Mirvis 1997; Kusstatscher and Cooper 2005; Sinkovics et al. 2011).

To be successful, acculturation necessitates social controls, such as information exchange, training, or social gatherings (Larsson and Lubatkin 2001). However, problems often arise when employees perceive differences in the acquisition partner's accustomed norms and values (Stahl et al. 2013). The resultant culture clashes manifest in stereotyping, polarizing differences and in degrading the acquisition partner's organizational culture (Marks and Mirvis 2011). This can make acquisitions extremely stressful (Ager 2011) and highlight an in-group–out-group bias; *us* versus *them* (Menges and Kilduff 2015). Nevertheless, positive emotions are essential for successful integration (Birkinshaw et al. 2000; Kusstatscher and Cooper 2005).

4 What Is This Book About?

4.1 Research Agenda

Although emotions have lately received much attention in the acquisition literature, the discussion remains somewhat inconsistent and undertheorized (Reus 2012; Zagelmeyer et al. 2016). A key limitation is the negative bias in the existing research. The focus has largely been on overcoming issues like stress, change resistance and fears of losing one's job (e.g. Marks and Mirvis 2001; Kusstatscher and Cooper 2005; Sinkovics et al. 2011). Unfortunately, the conclusion has been that emotions cause poor organizational outcomes, are generally negative, appear largely in the acquired organization and are triggered by personal circumstances (Graebner et al. 2017). Nevertheless, it has been found that acquisition-related emotions can also be positive and lead to positive outcomes, such as identification (Kusstatscher 2006; Raitis et al. 2017). Thus, a more balanced view and increased conceptual clarity are necessary in order to further the agenda of emotion research during acquisitions.

Previous research has also failed to pinpoint how collective emotions can be managed following acquisitions (Huy 2012). Indeed, the change management literature altogether lacks depth in terms of understanding how emotions emerge in and influence social structures (Zietsma et al.

2019). Thus, active emotion management during organizational change periods—such as post-acquisition integration—necessitates further research (Steigenberger 2015). Similarly, the influence of individual and group emotions on organizational spheres lacks understanding (Ashkanasy et al. 2017; Parke and Seo 2017). This book furthers this research agenda through clarifying concepts and their interrelations. The aim of this book is to offer scholars an increased theoretical understanding and examples of scientific rigour in emotion-centric empirical research. For practitioners, this book offers practical emotion management guidelines based on real-world evidence, designed to ease organizational change processes.

4.2 Three Single-Case Studies

This book introduces three case studies on employee experiences following acquisitions (see Table 1.1 for an overview of the cases and relevant methodology). As emotion is a highly subjective and context-specific topic of research, the immediate surroundings and personal backgrounds of individuals inevitably influence their emotional experiences. Thus, it is desirable to collect data from various organizations and at different organizational levels. This makes the case-study methodology particularly applicable, as it allows for the examination of real-life phenomena in their natural surroundings, connecting empirical evidence with explanatory theory (Flyvbjerg 2001; Welch and Piekkari 2017). A single case maximizes the richness of contextualized descriptions (Dyer and Wilkins 1991) and enables the collection of extensive data (Yin 2012) from multiple informants, yet describes a single setting (Fletcher and Plakoyiannaki 2011). This enables interpretive sensemaking (Welch et al. 2011), allowing for both a theoretical and practical depth of understanding. The purpose of these cases is to illustrate settings where the phenomena of interest naturally occur (cf. Stake 1995). Thus, this book utilizes three separate single-case studies, with a concluding cross-case analysis. Through this combination of single and multiple case designs, this book offers both thick contextualization and an enhanced potential for transferability (Fletcher and Plakoyiannaki 2011).

The three case contexts introduced in this book are both similar enough to offer comparable findings, but, at the same time, they are diverse enough to enable naturalistic generalizations to be made (cf. Flyvbjerg 2001; Ruddin 2006). Each represents traditional industries, but the companies were of different sizes and the cases provide different viewpoints on

Table 1.1 The three case studies

	Industry	*Acquirer*	*Target*	*Deal*	*Methodology*	*Data*
Chapter 2	Manufacturing	Finnish, medium-sized, family-owned LLC	German, medium-sized, investment company-owned GmbH	Friendly acquisition with a merger approach to integration	Mixed method	Three employee satisfaction surveys (2015, 2016 and 2018), 13 semi-structured interviews (2016) and one occasion of participant observation (2015)
Chapter 3	Manufacturing	German, large, global group GmbH	Finnish, small LLC	Friendly acquisition with a slow integration approach	Mixed method	26 interviews (2017 and 2018), 61 diary entries (2017 and 2018), employee satisfaction survey (2017)
Chapter 4	High-tech	Finnish, small LLC, which has moved from family ownership to investment company ownership	Several small Finnish LLCs	Friendly acquisitions with initial autonomy and later simultaneous integration	Qualitative	24 semi-structured interviews utilizing the Critical Incident Technique (2019)

power within M&As. The first case study includes data from both acquisition partners, the second explores emotions in the target company, while the third focuses on the buying organization. In each case study, the data is widely collected from all hierarchical levels in the involved organizations, thus extending our understanding beyond the customary stance of exploring middle- and top-management perspectives. Furthermore, two of the cases are international, whereas one is domestic. Details of each case, including the data collection and analysis, are provided in the subsequent chapters.

The first case study in Chap. 2 reveals how positivity can be found in a merger of equals. This chapter highlights how, through management interventions, positive emotions can be generated and fostered during post-acquisition integration. Mergers of equals are rare among acquisitions, making this case unique and interesting. The findings are based on interviews and employee satisfaction surveys conducted in both involved organizations, centring on exploring the emotions that arise when two organizations come together to set up a new entity. The second case study in Chap. 3 explores finding unity in a more traditional acquisition setting, where the parent company enforced changes in the new subsidiary. The discussion centres on finding unity when the *us* versus *them* thinking that is common in acquisitions is heightened. This setting often triggers negative protectionist attitudes in the target company employees. However, with careful emotion management, the integration process can become swifter and smoother. The findings stem from interviews, memo-like diaries and an employee satisfaction survey. The third case study in Chap. 4 discusses continuity from the viewpoint of a serial acquirer. The acquiring company perspective is rare among the acquisition literature as most studies tend to focus on the acquired company. The data comes from a 30-year-old company, which, during its life course, has undergone both a change from family ownership to investor ownership and rapid growth through a series of acquisitions, joining forces with smaller competitors. During this turmoil, the organizational identity and strategy changed, causing several emotional reactions.

5 Conclusion

This introduction has outlined the key theories that the following chapters build on: cognitive appraisal and affective events. In the following chapters, the three case studies that were briefly introduced above will be used to highlight how this theoretical insight helps us to understand post-acquisition integration from a more human-centric perspective. The concluding chapter recaps the findings from each case study and provides scholars with a map of interconnected concepts and their relation to acquisition research, aiming at increasing scientific rigour in future acquisition research when considering employee emotions.

References

Ager, D. L. (2011). The emotional impact and behavioral consequences of post-M&A integration: An ethnographic case study in the software industry. *Journal of Contemporary Ethnography, 40*(2), 199–230. https://doi.org/10.1177/0891241610387134.

Arnold, M. (1960). *Emotion and personality. Volume I: Psychological aspects.* New York: Columbia University Press.

Ashkanasy, N. M. (2003). Emotions in organizations: A multi-level perspective. *Research in Multi-Level Issues, 2,* 9–54. https://doi.org/10.1016/S1475-9144(03)02002-2.

Ashkanasy, N. M., & Dorris, A. D. (2017). Emotions in the workplace. *Annual Review of Organizational Psychology and Organizational Behavior, 4,* 67–90.

Ashkanasy, N. M., Humphrey, R. H., & Huy, Q. N. (2017). Integrating emotions and affect in theories of management. *Academy of Management Review, 42*(2), 175–189.

Basch, J., & Fisher, C. (1998, August). *Affective events–emotions matrix: A classification of work events and associated emotions.* Paper presented at the First Conference on Emotions in Organizational Life, San Diego, California. School of Business Discussion Papers 65: Bond University.

Ben-Ze'ev, A., & Krebs, A. (2018). Preface. In A. Ben-Ze'ev & A. Krebs (Eds.), *Philosophy of emotion.* Milton Park: Routledge.

Birkinshaw, J., Bresman, H., & Håkanson, L. (2000). Managing the post-acquisition integration process: How the human integration and task integration processes interact to foster value creation. *Journal of Management Studies, 37*(3), 395–425. https://doi.org/10.1111/1467-6486.00186.

Bowen, J. L. (2014). Emotion in organizations: Resources for business educators. *Journal of Management Education, 38*(1), 114–142. https://doi.org/10.1177/1052562913488110.

Cabanac, M. (2002). What is emotion? *Behavioural Processes, 60*(2), 69–83. https://doi.org/10.1016/S0376-6357(02)00078-5.

Carrera, P., & Oceja, L. (2009). Drawing mixed emotions: Sequential or simultaneous experiences? *Cognition & Emotion, 21*(2), 422–441. https://doi.org/10.1080/02699930600557904.

Cartwright, S., & Cooper, C. L. (1995). Organizational marriage: "Hard" versus "soft" issues? *Personnel Review, 24*(3), 32–42. https://doi.org/10.1108/00483489510089632.

Casper, A., Tremmel, S., & Sonnentag, S. (2019). The power of affect: A three-wave panel study on reciprocal relationships between work events and affect at work. *Journal of Occupational and Organizational Psychology, 92*(2), 436–460. https://doi.org/10.1111/joop.12255.

Clarke, N., & Salleh, N. M. (2011). Emotions and their management during a merger in Brunei. *Human Resource Development International, 14*(3), 291–304. https://doi.org/10.1080/13678868.2011.585064.

Cornelius, R. R. (2006). Magda Arnold's Thomistic theory of emotion, the self-ideal, and the moral dimension of appraisal. *Cognition & Emotion, 20*(7), 976–1000. https://doi.org/10.1080/02699930600616411.

Datta, D. K. (1991). Organizational fit and acquisition performance: Effects of post-acquisition integration. *Strategic Management Journal, 12*(4), 281–297. https://doi.org/10.1002/smj.4250120404.

Durand, M. (2016). Employing critical incident technique as one way to display the hidden aspects of post-merger integration. *International Business Review, 25*(1), 87–102. https://doi.org/10.1016/j.ibusrev.2015.05.003.

Dyer, W. G., & Wilkins, A. L. (1991). Better stories, not better constructs, to generate better theory: A rejoinder to Eisenhardt. *Academy of Management Review, 16*(3), 613–619. https://doi.org/10.5465/AMR.1991.4279492.

Ekman, P., & Cordaro, D. (2011). What is meant by calling emotions basic. *Emotion Review, 3*(4), 364–370. https://doi.org/10.1177/1754073911410740.

Fink, G., & Yolles, M. (2015). Collective emotion regulation in an organisation: A plural agency with cognition and affect. *Journal of Organizational Change Management, 28*(5), 832–871. https://doi.org/10.1108/JOCM-09-2014-0179.

Fisher, C. (2002). Antecedents and consequences of real-time affective reactions at work. *Motivation and Emotion, 26*(1), 3–30.

Fletcher, M., & Plakoyiannaki, E. (2011). Case selection in international business: Key issues and common misconceptions. In R. Piekkari & C. Welch (Eds.), *Rethinking the case study in international business and management research* (pp. 171–191). Cheltenham: Edward Elgar.

Flyvbjerg, B. (2001). *Making social science matter: Why social inquiry fails and how it can succeed again*. Cambridge: Cambridge University Press.

Fredrickson, B. L. (2001). The role of positive emotions in positive psychology. *American Psychologist, 56*(3), 218–226. https://doi.org/10.1037/0003-066X.56.3.218.

Fugate, M., Kinicki, A., & Scheck, C. (2002). Coping with an organizational merger over four stages. *Personnel Psychology, 55*(4), 905–928.

Goldenberg, A., Saguy, T., & Halperin, E. (2014). How group-based emotions are shaped by collective emotions: Evidence for emotional transfer and emotional burden. *Journal of Personality and Social Psychology, 107*(4), 581–596. https://doi.org/10.1037/a0037462.

Gordon, R. (1987). *The structure of emotions: Investigations in cognitive philosophy.* Cambridge: Cambridge University Press.

Graebner, M. E., Heimeriks, K. H., Huy, Q. N., & Vaara, E. (2017). The process of postmerger integration: A review and agenda for future research. *Academy of Management Annals, 11*(1), 1–32. https://doi.org/10.5465/annals.2014.0078.

Guerrero, L., Andersen, P., & Trost, M. (1996). Communication and emotion: Basic concepts and approaches. In P. Andersen & L. Guerrero (Eds.), *Handbook of communication and emotion: Research, theory, applications, and contexts* (pp. 3–27). San Diego, CA: Academic.

Gunkel, M., Schlaegel, C., Rossteutscher, T., & Wolff, B. (2015). The human aspect of cross-border acquisition outcomes: The role of management practices, employee emotions, and national culture. *International Business Review, 24*(3), 394–408. https://doi.org/10.1016/j.ibusrev.2014.09.001.

Harikkala-Laihinen, R. (2019). *The power of positivity: How employee emotions and interaction can benefit cross-border acquisitions.* Turku: University of Turku.

Huy, Q. N. (2012). Emotions in strategic organization: Opportunities for impactful research. *Strategic Organization, 10*(3), 240–247. https://doi.org/10.1177/1476127012453107.

Izard, C. (1972). *The psychology of emotions.* New York: Plenum Press.

Izard, C. (2007). Basic emotions, natural kinds, emotion schemas, and a new paradigm. *Perspectives on Psychological Science, 2*(3), 260–280. https://doi.org/10.1111/j.1745-6916.2007.00044.x.

Karlgaard, R. (2014). *Soft edge: Where great companies find lasting success.* San Francisco, CA: Jossey-Bass.

Kemper, T. D. (2002). Predicting emotions in groups: Some lessons from September 11. *The Sociological Review, 50*(S2), 53–68.

Kiefer, T. (2002). Understanding the emotional experience of organizational change: Evidence from a merger. *Advances in Developing Human Resources, 4*(1), 39–61.

Kiefer, T. (2005). Feeling bad: Antecedents and consequences of negative emotions in ongoing change. *Journal of Organizational Behavior, 26*(8), 875–897.

Kleinginna, P. R., & Kleinginna, A. M. (1981). A categorized list of emotion definitions, with suggestions for a consensual definition. *Motivation and Emotion, 5*(4), 345–379. https://doi.org/10.1007/BF00992553.

Kusstatscher, V. (2006). Cultivating positive emotions in mergers and acquisitions. *Advances in Mergers and Acquisitions, 5*, 91–103.

Kusstatscher, V., & Cooper, C. (2005). *Managing emotions in mergers and acquisitions*. Cheltenham: Edward Elgar.

Larsson, R., & Lubatkin, M. (2001). Achieving acculturation in mergers and acquisitions: An international case survey. *Human Relations, 54*(12), 1573–1607. https://doi.org/10.1177/00187267015412002.

Lazarus, R. (1991). *Emotion and adaptation*. New York: Oxford University Press.

Marks, M. L., & Mirvis, P. H. (1997). Revisiting the merger syndrome: Crisis management. Part 2. *Mergers and Acquisitions, 31*(6), 21–27.

Marks, M. L., & Mirvis, P. H. (2001). Making mergers and acquisitions work: Strategic and psychological preparation. *Academy of Management Executive, 15*(2), 80–94.

Marks, M. L., & Mirvis, P. H. (2011). A framework for the human resources role in managing culture in mergers and acquisitions. *Human Resource Management, 50*(6), 859–877. https://doi.org/10.1002/hrm.20445.

Menges, J. I., & Kilduff, M. (2015). Group emotions: Cutting the gordian knots concerning terms, levels of analysis, and processes. *Academy of Management Annals, 9*(1), 845–928. https://doi.org/10.1080/19416520.2015.1033148

Mignonac, K., & Herrbach, O. (2004). Linking work events, affective states, and attitudes: An empirical study of managers' emotions. *Journal of Business and Psychology, 19*(2), 221–240.

Morgeson, F., Mitchell, T., & Liu, D. (2015). Event system theory: An event-oriented approach to the organizational sciences. *Academy of Management Review, 40*(4), 515–537.

Nahavandi, A., & Malekzadeh, A. R. (1988). Acculturation in mergers and acquisitions. *Academy of Management Review, 13*(1), 79–90. https://doi.org/10.5465/AMR.1988.4306790.

Nussbaum, M. (2004). Emotions as judgments of value and importance. In R. C. Solomon (Ed.), *Thinking about feeling* (pp. 183–199). Oxford: Oxford University Press.

Oreg, S., Bartunek, J. M., Lee, G., & Do, B. (2018). An affect-based model of recipients' responses to organizational change events. *Academy of Management Review, 43*(1), 65–86. https://doi.org/10.5465/amr.2014.0335.

Parke, M. R., & Seo, M.-G. (2017). The role of affect climate in organizational effectiveness. *Academy of Management Review, 42*(2), 334–360.

Raitis, J., Harikkala-Laihinen, R., Hassett, M., & Nummela, N. (2017). Finding positivity during a major organizational change: In search of triggers of employees' positive perceptions and feelings. In W. Zerbe, C. Härtel, N. Ashkanasy, & L. Petitta (Eds.), *Emotions and identity: Research on emotion in organizations* (Vol. 13, pp. 3–16). https://doi.org/10.1108/S1746-979120170000013001.

Raitis, J., Harikkala-Laihinen, R., Hassett, M., & Nummela, N. (2018). *Socio-cultural integration in mergers and acquisitions: The Nordic approach*. Cham: Palgrave Pivot.

Reus, T. H. (2012). Culture's consequences for emotional attending during cross-border acquisition implementation. *Journal of World Business, 47*(3), 342–351. https://doi.org/10.1016/j.jwb.2011.05.002.

Rottig, D., Reus, T. H., & Tarba, S. (2013). The impact of culture on mergers and acquisitions: A third of a century of research. *Advances in Mergers and Acquisitions, 12*, 135–172. https://doi.org/10.1108/MRR-09-2015-0216.

Ruddin, L. P. (2006). You can generalize stupid! Social scientists, Bent Flyvbjerg, and case study methodology. *Qualitative Inquiry, 12*(4), 797–812. https://doi.org/10.1177/1077800406288622.

Russell, J. A. (2003). Core affect and the psychological construction of emotion. *Psychological Review, 110*(1), 145–172. https://doi.org/10.1037/0033-295X.110.1.145.

Russell, J. A., & Carroll, J. M. (1999). On the bipolarity of positive and negative affect. *Psychological Bulletin, 125*(1), 3–30. https://doi.org/10.1037/0033-2909.125.1.3.

Sarala, R. M., Vaara, E., & Junni, P. (2019). Beyond merger syndrome and cultural differences: New avenues for research on the "human side" of global mergers and acquisitions (M&As). *Journal of World Business, 54*(4), 307–321. https://doi.org/10.1016/j.jwb.2017.10.001.

Scherer, K. R. (2005). What are emotions? And how can they be measured? *Social Science Information, 44*(4), 695–729. https://doi.org/10.1177/0539018405058216.

Scherer, K. R., & Moors, A. (2019). The emotion process: Event appraisal and component differentiation. *Annual Review of Psychology, 70*, 719–745.

Sinkovics, R. R., Zagelmeyer, S., & Kusstatscher, V. (2011). Between merger and syndrome: The intermediary role of emotions in four cross-border M&As. *International Business Review, 20*(1), 27–47. https://doi.org/10.1016/j.ibusrev.2010.05.002.

Smollan, R. (2006). Minds, hearts and deeds: Cognitive, affective and behavioural responses to change. *Journal of Change Management, 6*(2), 143–158. https://doi.org/10.1080/14697010600725400.

Solomon, R. C. (2003). I. Emotions, thoughts and feelings: What is a "cognitive theory" of the emotions and does it neglect affectivity? *Royal Institute of Philosophy Supplement, 52*(2003), 1–18. https://doi.org/10.1017/S1358246100007864.

Solomon, R. C. (2008). The philosophy of emotion. In M. Lewis, J. M. Haviland-Jones, & L. Feldman Barrett (Eds.), *Handbook of emotions* (pp. 3–16). New York: Guilford.

Stahl, G., Angwin, D. N., Very, P., Gomes, E., Weber, Y., Tarba, S. Y., et al. (2013). Sociocultural integration in mergers and acquisitions: Unresolved paradoxes and directions for future research. *Thunderbird International Business Review, 55*(4), 333–356. https://doi.org/10.1002/tie.

Stake, R. (1995). *The art of case study research.* Thousand Oaks, CA: Sage.

Steigenberger, N. (2015). Emotions in sensemaking: A change management perspective. *Journal of Organizational Change Management, 28*(3), 432–451. https://doi.org/10.1108/JOCM-05-2014-0095.

Wang, Q., Clegg, J., Gajewska-De Mattos, H., & Buckley, P. (2018). The role of emotions in intercultural business communication: Language standardization in the context of international knowledge transfer. *Journal of World Business.* https://doi.org/10.1016/j.jwb.2018.11.003.

Watson, D., & Tellegen, A. (1985). Toward a consensual structure of mood. *Psychological Bulletin, 98*(2), 219–235. https://doi.org/10.1037/0033-2909.98.2.219.

Weiss, H., & Beal, D. (2005). The effect of affect in organizational settings: Reflections on affective events theory. In N. M. Ashkanasy, W. Zerbe, & C. Härtel (Eds.), *Research on emotion in organizations* (Vol. 1, pp. 1–21). Bingley: Emerald. https://doi.org/10.1016/S1746-9791(05)01101-6.

Weiss, H., & Cropanzano, R. (1996). Affective events theory: A theoretical discussion of the structure, causes and consequences of affective experiences at work. In B. M. Staw & L. L. Cummings (Eds.), *Research in organizational behavior: An annual series of analytical essays and critical reviews* (Vol. 18, pp. 1–74). JAI Press and Elsevier Science.

Welch, C., & Piekkari, R. (2017). How should we (not) judge the "quality" of qualitative research? A re-assessment of current evaluative criteria in international business. *Journal of World Business, 52*(5), 714–725. https://doi.org/10.1016/j.jwb.2017.05.007.

Welch, C., Piekkari, R., Plakoyiannaki, E., & Paavilainen-Mäntymäki, E. (2011). Theorising from case studies: Towards a pluralist future for international business research. *Journal of International Business Studies, 42*(5), 740–762. https://doi.org/10.1057/jibs.2010.55.

Wilkinson, R., & Pickett, K. (2010). *The spirit level: Why equality is better for everyone.* London: Penguin.

Yin, R. (2012). *Applications of case study research* (3rd ed.). Thousand Oaks, CA: Sage.

Zagelmeyer, S., Sinkovics, R. R., Sinkovics, N., & Kusstatscher, V. (2016). Exploring the link between management communication and emotions in mergers and acquisitions. *Canadian Journal of Administrative Sciences, 35*(1), 93–106.

Zietsma, C., Toubiana, M., Voronov, M., & Roberts, A. (2019). *Emotions in organization theory.* Cambridge: Cambridge University Press.

CHAPTER 2

Finding Positivity in a Merger of Equals

Riikka Harikkala-Laihinen, Niina Nummela, Melanie Hassett, and Johanna Raitis

Abstract This chapter highlights how, through management interventions, positive emotions can be generated and fostered during post-acquisition integration. The findings are based on a Finnish–German acquisition completed in late 2013. Data collection via interviews and employee satisfaction surveys conducted in both involved organizations centred on exploring the emotions that arise when two organizations come together to set up a new entity. The integration setting represents a merger of equals, making this case unique and particularly interesting. The findings suggest that positive emotions, such as happiness and pride, have an engaging effect, motivating employees to work towards change. To cultivate post-acquisition positivity, organizations can offer employees

R. Harikkala-Laihinen (✉) • N. Nummela • J. Raitis
Turku School of Economics, University of Turku, Turku, Finland
e-mail: riikka.harikkala-laihinen@utu.fi

M. Hassett
Sheffield University Management School, Sheffield, UK

R. Harikkala-Laihinen, *Managing Emotions in Organizations*,
https://doi.org/10.1007/978-3-030-60567-4_2

positive emotion triggers, such as experiences of ownership and a compelling vision of the future of the company.

Keywords Positive organizational scholarship • Change management • Merger of equals

1 Introduction

Over the past three decades or so, the human side of acquisitions has received increasing attention (e.g. Cartwright and Cooper 1993; Sarala et al. 2019). The focus of this research stream has been on understanding acquisitions as softer human processes instead of just as hard cold facts (Cartwright and Cooper 1995). This growing body of literature argues that acquisition failure is often caused by sociocultural challenges during integration (e.g. Birkinshaw et al. 2000; Marks and Mirvis 2011; Raitis et al. 2018). These challenges often emerge from an in-group–out-group bias: *us* versus *them* thinking triggered by uncertainty during change and causing protectionist attitudes (Menges and Kilduff 2015). Consequently, defensive actions can culminate in a polarization of perceived differences between the acquisition partners, hence complicating integration (Marks and Mirvis 2011). Thus, collaboration and inclusion are key elements of successful integration (Harikkala-Laihinen et al. 2018).

Unfortunately, the previous literature concludes that emotions following acquisitions are mainly negative, emerge predominantly in the acquired company and are prompted by personal circumstances. Thus, emotions are assumed to cause poor organizational outcomes following acquisitions (Graebner et al. 2017). However, acquisitions can also raise positive emotions, such as happiness or pride (Kusstatscher 2006), and can have positive outcomes, such as identification with the new post-acquisition company (Raitis et al. 2017). Accordingly, the purpose of this chapter is to explore the emergence of positive emotions during post-acquisition integration. More particularly, this chapter asks (1) *What constitutes positive change management following a cross-border acquisition?* and (2) *How can positive change management ease post-acquisition integration?* To answer these questions, this chapter adopts a positive organizational scholarship (POS) lens. POS highlights positive human potential through an emphasis on the enablers, motivations and effects of positive organizational phenomena. In the organizational context, POS illustrates how positive contexts and dynamics are connected to positive states in individuals, groups and organizations (Cameron et al. 2003).

Through the POS lens, this chapter offers novel insights into how to manage a major organizational change in a positive way. The findings show that when positive emotions emerge and are harnessed to engage employees in post-acquisition change, the integration will be swifter and smoother. In addition, generating positive emotions eases alleviating the negative emotions that are an inherent part of the uncertainty following acquisitions. Thus, generating positivity following acquisitions can be a key means towards more successful integration.

2 Positive Organizational Change

2.1 Positive Organizational Scholarship

POS encourages scholars to highlight unexpectedly positive contexts (Cameron et al. 2003). POS focuses on organizational success under the influence of positive leadership, positive relationships, positive communication and a positive climate (Cameron 2012). Generating positive emotions is a central concern in POS because positive emotions may improve organizational outcomes (Cameron et al. 2003). Emphasizing the positive over the negative has the capacity to increase human thriving (Cameron 2017). This is because positive emotions broaden through patterns and enhance creativity, widening our information-processing ability. Such positive experiences build over time, and start outlasting the experienced emotion, turning into a personal reserve of resources we can tap into when faced with threats. Similarly, accumulated positive resources help us regulate negative experiences, thus increasing our overall emotional well-being and psychological resilience (Fredrickson 2001, 2013).

Apart from building a positive personal reserve, positivity can enhance organizational success. Organizational positivity is essential in creating a work climate which generates and encourages positive behaviour (Luthans and Youssef 2007). Similarly, positivity can increase employee engagement and thereby ease organizational change (Avey et al. 2008). Nevertheless, it must be noted that POS does not claim that organizations can or should achieve perfect happiness and harmony. Instead, POS postulates that simply seeking to neutralize negative outcomes is less beneficial than actively striving towards positive outcomes. A positive outcome in POS terms can be anything from improved organizational performance to positive actions or attitudes (Roberts 2006).

A key argument of POS is that positive organizational states are not achieved by merely reversing negativity (Roberts 2006). This notion has led international business and management scholars to note the negative bias in existing discussions on diversity, distance and foreignness. The existing literature largely emphasizes the negative aspects, which can direct attention away from understanding the potential benefits (Stahl et al. 2016). However, focusing on positivity can enable overcoming the liability of foreignness and can encourage particularly beneficial outcomes, beyond solving immediate problems (Cameron 2017). In order to overcome the pejorative nature of existing cross-cultural research, emphasize possible positive outcomes and explore experiences in depth in their natural context (cf. Stahl and Tung 2015), this chapter adopts a POS lens to post-acquisition change.

2.2 *Positive Change*

Although traditionally considered a practice of rationality, management includes an emotional element. This emotional element can be particularly relevant in change management because employees are more disposed to change when it triggers positive emotions (Karp 2004). This highlights management as commitment-building rather than controlling and emphasizes the managers' role in promoting change receptiveness (Caldwell 2003).

Deriving from seeing positive as goal-congruent and therefore pleasing, positive organizational change refers to change which is affirmative in terms of employee responses and organizational outcomes (Avey et al. 2008). Human beings possess an innate tendency towards positive change. However, as we grow older, we become more receptive to negative triggers (situations or events that trigger negative emotions), which overpowers the positivity trait. Consequently, emphasizing positive emotion triggers during change may be essential (Cameron 2008). Whereas negative emotions can activate instinctive fight-or-flight reactions, positive emotions broaden thought patterns, thereby encouraging more positive attitudes also towards change (Fredrickson 2001).

Nevertheless, employees often have distinctively negative reactions towards change. Such change resistance is caused by an aversion to the unknown and is thus an emotional reaction towards an unclear future (Dhingra and Punia 2016). Change resistance often generates negative attitudes or detrimental behaviour towards change (e.g. Waddell and Sohal 1998), but creating positive emotions regarding change can help overcome such resistance (Dhingra and Punia 2016). Thus, if companies are able to establish a positive climate surrounding change, they can help their employees overcome change-related anxiety (Birkinshaw et al. 2000; cf. Bar-tal et al. 2007; Fredrickson 2013).

An organizational climate means "the collective mood of organizational members toward their jobs, the organization, and management" (Ashkanasy 2003, p. 38). It connotes the visible part of the organization's culture (Momeni 2009) and includes the organization's emotional climate—a felt working atmosphere. An emotional climate is visible in the overarching collective emotional states that emerge through social interaction within an organization (DeRivera and Páez 2007). A positive climate is highly beneficial for change (Vacharkulksemsuk et al. 2010) as it enhances organizational identification and promotes collaboration (Fischer and Manstead 2008). An organization's emotional climate is considered positive when managers are able to take employees' personal growth and emotional needs into consideration and encourage employees to share positive emotions (Ozcelik et al. 2008). Thus, a positive climate does not indicate a lack of negative sentiments, but the greater power of positive features such as security and trust (Bar-tal et al. 2007).

2.3 Managing Positive Change

One of the most popular frameworks of organizational change was established by Kotter (1995), who emphasizes the necessity of a sense of urgency, a group to lead change, creating and communicating a vision to drive change efforts, empowering others to reach the vision, setting up interim objectives, reinvigorating the project continuously and institutionalizing new behaviours. Whetten and Cameron (2011) simplify these eight steps into five key management activities to create positive change: establishing a climate of positivity, creating readiness for change, articulating a vision of abundance, generating commitment to that vision and institutionalizing the change.

In order to create a positive change climate, managers should focus on employee contentment, efficient physical work environments and encouraging leadership (Maimone and Sinclair 2010). This can include being sensitive to employees' emotional needs, offering positive encouragement, or building active initiatives to encourage the emergence of a pleasant working atmosphere (Ozcelik et al. 2008). Building a positive change climate is important because a positive climate is likely to increase employees' positive emotions and thereby encourage positive organizational behaviour (Bar-tal et al. 2007). Companies often only focus on alleviating negativity, but because emotions are contagious, an increase in positivity leads to even more positivity (Hatfield et al. 1994; cf. Fredrickson 2013). Furthermore, studies have shown that a healthy happy employee is an effective employee (e.g. Russell 2008). This is why it is better to boost positivity rather than just alleviate negativity during change (cf. Dhingra and Punia 2016).

In creating readiness, communicating the importance and urgency of the change is the key to engaging employees. However, for change to be successful, a vision of abundance—or a positive future—must be established, and commitment to that vision generated (Whetten and Cameron 2011; cf. Kotter 1995). In motivating employees' engagement through these actions, managers need to reflect on their own actions. Employees tend to mirror their managers' emotions, meaning that the simplest way for managers to increase positivity is to express positive emotions towards change. Indeed, managers' emotional displays when communicating with employees may be crucial (Hatfield et al. 1994; cf. Ashkanasy and Daus 2002). Managers' positive emotions can generate further positive emotions in employees, encouraging behaviour which is congruent with organizational change objectives (Newcombe and Ashkanasy 2002; Bono and Ilies 2006; Johnson 2008; Gooty et al. 2010).

In addition to portraying positive emotions, managers can take an active role in facilitating change-related discussions, promoting agreement, encouraging thinking, as well as persuading and engaging employees regarding change-congruent behaviour. In order to succeed in promoting positivity towards change, managers can allow their passion towards the change objectives to show in their communications, portray a clear target and delegate tasks to ensure sufficient change resources. Moreover, managers should walk the talk, evaluate ongoing change processes objectively and promptly reward success (Cameron and Green 2012). Indeed, an inability to communicate the vision driving the change successfully and not removing potential obstacles for that vision are key failure factors in change management (Kotter 1995). In institutionalizing the change, creating momentum is key. This is when ownership of the change should, ideally, switch from the managers to the engaged employees (Whetten and Cameron 2011). Institutionalization principally reflects the durability of the change; a commitment to the current state (Armenakis et al. 1999). Interim objectives that create feelings of success are an important driver towards overall change. Such objectives should, in time, turn into the new daily routine, thus institutionalizing the change (Kotter 1995).

To cope with managing positive change, the most successful leaders appear to have high emotional intelligence (e.g. Goleman 1998; Gardner and Stough 2002; Ovans 2015). Emotional intelligence means the "ability to monitor one's own and others' feelings and emotions, to discriminate among them and to use this information to guide one's thinking and actions" (Salovey and Mayer 1990, p. 189). An emotionally intelligent individual can thus understand and explain their own and others' emotions as well as recognize the influence of emotions on thought (Mayer and Caruso 2002). Emotional intelligence is particularly helpful for change management (Mayer and Caruso 2002) because managers with high emotional intelligence can recognize and understand employee emotions as well as react to or even modify these emotions in order to facilitate change (George 2000). High emotional intelligence can help with detecting and managing employees' emotions better, creating and maintaining optimism and excitement, managing employee reactions, honing decision-making, maintaining a strong organizational identity and culture, and guiding in forming compelling goals (George 2000).

2.4 *Positive Post-Acquisition Change*

Positive emotions in particular have been found to be crucial for successful integration (Birkinshaw et al. 2000; Kusstatscher and Cooper 2005). Whereas negative emotions can strengthen employee identification with the pre-acquisition organization, positive emotions may generate a stronger identity and unity in the post-acquisition organization (Kusstatscher and Cooper 2005; Raitis et al. 2017). In addition, following a friendly acquisition, the change climate is more likely to give rise to feelings of security. However, a hostile takeover is more likely to lead to a climate of fear (Fink and Yolles 2015). Table 2.1 links the notions of positive change and emotionally intelligent leadership to integration management.

Based on the notions of emotionally intelligent leadership and positive change, this chapter suggests that managing positive post-acquisition change centres on employee emotions. The focus on positivity emphasizes its importance in furthering post-acquisition integration (Birkinshaw et al. 2000). In this context, adopting the positive change management steps and portraying emotional intelligence help managers facilitate change. This implies identifying and responding to employee emotions, encouraging positivity, increasing engagement and excitement, endorsing an advantageous future vision of the joint organization and increasing employee commitment to the integrated rather than to the pre-acquisition organization.

Table 2.1 Managing positive post-acquisition change

Positive change	*Emotional intelligence*	*Managing integration*
Establish a climate of positivity	Detect and manage employees' emotions better	Detect and understand employee emotions in order to encourage positivity
Create readiness for change	Create and maintain excitement and optimism	Communicate the positive aspects of integration, creating a sense of excitement and readiness
Articulate a vision of abundance	Form compelling goals	Form a compelling vision of the future of the integrated company
Generate commitment	Detect and understand others' emotions	Respond to employees' emotions in ways that encourage commitment to the integrated company
Institutionalize the change	Maintain a strong organizational culture	Strengthen the achieved integration through encouraging employees to identify with the new organization

3 Method

3.1 A Merger of Equals[1]

Established in the mid-1900s, Alpha had become known as a Finnish family-owned company with international industrial operations to develop, manufacture and market technologically advanced user-friendly products. Alpha was considered a reliable supplier both in Finland and abroad—particularly in the Nordic countries. In late 2013, Alpha acquired Beta, a German competitor, which had formerly also been family-owned but had since been bought by a capital investor. At the time of the deal, Alpha employed some 800 workers, whereas Beta employed approximately 600. The deal was friendly, and because the two companies had complementary product lines, were similar in size, and were balanced in terms of market power, Alpha chose to pursue a best-of-both-worlds approach to integration, in effect resembling a merger of equals (cf. Haspeslagh and Jemison 1991; Cartwright and Cooper 1993). The new name of the joint company would be Alpha Group, highlighting Alpha's ownership but, at the same time, emphasizing equality across functions and locations.

[1]The data for this chapter has previously been discussed in Harikkala-Laihinen, R. (2019) *The power of positivity: How employee emotions and interaction can benefit cross-border acquisitions*. Turku: University of Turku.

Alpha Group's integration strategy was based on several projects, of which "Cultural integration and HR" is the focus of this chapter. The objectives of this integration project were to establish common values in the joint organization as well as to introduce a single Alpha Group company structure while maintaining the two brand names of Alpha and Beta. Work on the cultural issues only started in late 2014 when a cooperation agreement for data collection was reached. The goal was to form new organizational values to act as the foundation for a strong joint culture. The project started with identifying the existing work-related values at Alpha Group, which yielded four core values for the new company: courage, fairness, effectiveness and openness.

Each value was described in terms of internal and external relations, but the description remained abstract, so that employees could adopt them more easily. In order to encourage the practical application of the values, in early 2015, Alpha Group invited all employees to specific value workshops where the values were introduced and discussed based on the employees' perspectives. The workshops gathered a small (maximum 20) local group of people across organizational departments to interact with each other and breathe life into the values. The purpose of the workshops was to give employees examples of how the values could be incorporated in daily work.

3.2 Data Collection and Analysis

The Alpha Group case represents a single significant case (cf. Patton 2015), reflecting the strategic selection of a case, which is particularly helpful in increasing understanding but at the same time allowing for naturalistic generalizations to be made (cf. Flyvbjerg 2001; Ruddin 2006). Although the case is statistically atypical as it represents a merger of equals, it is particularly informative (cf. Fletcher and Plakoyiannaki 2011) and thus ensures the best illumination of the phenomenon of interest (cf. Stake 1995).

The main data for this chapter consists of three employee satisfaction surveys conducted in spring 2015, 2016, and 2018. The first survey explored employee opinions and emotions regarding the value workshops, the acquisition in general, as well as the integration that followed through open-ended questions. The response rate was approximately 50%, with 681 informants. In 2016, the employees were asked to describe their emotions regarding the deal again through an open-ended question. The response rate was 82%, with 1082 responses given. In 2018, the employees were asked both statistical and open-ended questions. First, the employees were asked to evaluate how well the objective of unification had been achieved. Second, the employees were asked to identify, on a five-point scale from *not at all* to *extremely*, which emotions they were experiencing, with options based on the previous surveys. In addition, the respondents could elaborate on their answers. The quantitative sections had 1069 respondents, of whom 400 made clarifying comments. This represents a response rate of 74% and 28%, respectively.

The 2015 and 2016 surveys were analysed both quantitatively and qualitatively. First, the responses were categorized numerically into 0 (no emotional content or missing response), 1 (negative emotional content), 2 (both negative and positive emotional content) and 3 (positive emotional content). The numeric codes were transferred to SPSS20 for descriptive statistical analysis. The responses containing emotional content (i.e. codes other than 0) were transferred to QSR NVivo for an in-depth qualitative understanding regarding the exact emotions and their triggers. The analysis followed the emotion categories of Lazarus (1993), which allows for the separation between the trigger and the emotion. Thus, a three-order structure was born; valence (positive or negative), emotion label and emotion trigger. The statistical responses for the 2018 survey were analysed again using the SPSS analysis process, whereas the elaborative qualitative responses were categorized into themes emerging from the responses in QSR NVivo.

In addition to the surveys, 13 interviews (Table 2.2) were conducted between late 2015 and mid-2016 in order to gain more in-depth accounts regarding the context and individual perceptions. The interviewees were the top-management team members (10), HR representatives (2) and the integration manager. Six interviews were conducted in Finland in Finnish, and seven in Germany in English. Due to distance, two interviews used Skype. All interviews were audio-recorded (altogether 830 minutes) and transcribed for analysis. The analysis was undertaken in QSR NVivo, where the data was categorized according to themes arising from theory (such as integration, the deal, emotions) as well as from the data (such as describing Alpha/Beta, challenges in the deal).

Finally, participant observation occurred in one of the value workshops organized in Finland in February 2015. During the workshop, the new values were introduced to the participants, engaging them in giving meaning to the values and helping them to adopt the values in their daily work. The observations were recorded as field notes. These field notes were used to inform the analysis of other datasets.

Table 2.2 Alpha Group interviews

Interviewee title	*Duration*	*Language*
CEO	99 min	Finnish
Vice President, Sales	56 min	English
Vice President, Product Management	74 min	Finnish
Internal Services Manager, Union Representative	51 min	English
Vice President, Sales in German-Speaking Areas	60 min	English
Vice President, Brand Management	68 min	English
Vice President, Purchasing and Logistics	55 min	English
Vice President, Manufacturing and IT	52 min	English
CFO	50 min	Finnish
Employee Representative	55 min	Finnish
HR Manager	56 min	Finnish
Vice President, Business Development and HR	66 min	Finnish
Integration Manager	90 min	Finnish

4 Finding Positivity at Alpha Group

4.1 Emotions at Alpha Group

At Alpha Group, employees were distinctly more disposed to change when it triggered positive emotions (cf. Karp 2004). Based on the categorization of Lazarus (1993), three positive emotions, four negative emotions and one mixed emotion arose. As emotions are dynamic, and bound in time and space, they also varied between individuals and the different data-collection time points (see Table 2.3 for an overview of the findings).

In the following, the positive and mixed emotions are explored first, and employees' negative experiences are considered afterwards. The following reflects the emotions and triggers found in the 2015 and 2016 employee satisfaction surveys when integration was still ongoing.

4.1.1 Positive Emotions

Happiness was among the most significant of the emotions experienced by the employees throughout the datasets. Happiness refers to making progress towards a personal goal or objective (Lazarus 1993). At Alpha Group, the value workshops triggered happiness in many ways; they created

Table 2.3 Emotions at Alpha Group

Valence	*Emotion*[a]	*Quotes 2015*	*Quotes 2016*	*Percentages and elaboration 2018*
Positive	Happiness	Absolutely positive, since the merger of two major brands and the combining of competencies offers good opportunities for tackling the challenges of the future	The sense of having a safe workplace is highly motivating	90% felt slightly, somewhat, significantly, or extremely happy
		The merger of both companies offers a great opportunity for efficiency, and for optimizing the processes in both companies	We have come with a good solid organization who knows what they are doing, and say what they are going to do and then does it. Open minded and down to earth	40% felt significantly or extremely happy
		At the time of the deal I thought that great, I am now part of a growing international company.	I am very glad, and I am very happy that the company is developing. Emotions: happiness, contentment, satisfaction, pride	Joy, because we are stronger together and can achieve more
		Substantial emotions and internal joy because the Alpha company is developing its strength in relation to our competition	I'm happy to belong to a large group, and be able to sell innovative products with attractive designs	Be a part of a large family-owned business
		When I heard the news, the feeling was that good, we are moving forward and creating a stronger foundation for business	Basically, only positive feelings. For example, how the competencies present on both sides are generating a lot of opportunities for all involved	
		Positive emotions based on trust and common business development	I like the two worlds united into one with all their little differences. That's why we are internally so strong, meaning in the YIN-YANG principle	
		The company's (group's) values feel like a strong foundation to stand on and the company's mission/vision is clear	I'm always happy about this, and feel very positive about the future	
		Very good feelings. The values that the company has adopted, and my own personal values are very much in line with each other, so this is good	Confidence that we are on the right track. Certainty of having a secure job in the future	
		It is fun and pleasant to work in a company that has a clear objective. It is very good for tomorrow that we have clear values	I feel happy to know I'm in a very good company, and will do my training there	

Relief	I feel more secure; namely, I am slowly developing confidence. A feeling is slowly developing, something like "having arrived"	Generally, the atmosphere is positive since the company probably would not have gone on without Alpha. Currently, we are stagnating	76% felt slightly, somewhat, significantly, or extremely relieved
	Reassured, somewhat more secure—good for working	In my view, the decision was correct for the Beta employees, and necessary for the continued existence of Beta	29% felt significantly or extremely relieved
	There was a certain tension, which is a logical consequence of major changes. There was good internal guidance, so that it quickly became clear how it would continue, which created a positive feeling	Not having to worry about my job	The needs of the Beta markets will now be strongly represented; the outlook through Finnish eyes only has ended
	With relief, the perspectives for the future look good	Less fear of the future than a few years back	Relieved to see that changes are underway
	On the one hand relief, to change over from investors to a traditional company	The recent merger first brought about uncertainty, there was a lack of confidence in the project. Now, two years on, trust has grown, inner peace is present with a certain level of security, so that we can now get on with the achievement of the goals	Relief, because we are on the right track
Pride	Pride, a feeling of success. We thought that the Alpha trademark would now spread better in Central Europe as well	On one hand I'm proud of such a huge organization specializing in faucet production for the whole of Europe	90% felt slightly, somewhat, significantly,, or extremely proud
	I'm proud to be part of this group!	Pride—companies with great potential	45% felt significantly or extremely proud
	Makes me proud to work at a company which values honesty and fairness! It's good that we have outspoken values in the company	Generally very good. The pride to work in a group that is advancing and specially for a prestigious brand	Through the merger with Alpha Group, we are now a part of an international company, which wants to become a leading provider of sanitary fittings in the near future. I feel proud to be able to work on this goal
	My feelings are only positive. We are now really an international company and it's something to be proud of	I am proud that we are represented on the market by such strong brand names	I think we're all proud to work for a company like Alpha Group
	I feel that I am in good hands at Alpha. They even let little workers know that they belong to the family, and that is something of which I am proud		

(*continued*)

Table 2.3 (continued)

Valence	*Emotion*[a]	*Quotes 2015*	*Quotes 2016*	*Percentages and elaboration 2018*
Negative	Anxiety	All new things are always suspicious at first	Despair. We still haven't managed to achieve common practices!	54% felt slightly, somewhat, significantly, or extremely anxious
		I was a bit frightened when I heard the news	Decisions are taken globally, the German market is no longer the main priority. This is a source of concern to me	11% felt significantly or extremely anxious
		At first I was suspicious as to what the future will bring	Concerned about how the various units will retain their expertise	Anxiety—a clash of the Finnish and the German management methods. The visions do not seem fully compatible
		Confusion and uncertainty	It sometimes seems that politics/looking after one's own interests comes before the benefit of the company	I see it as a great challenge to also adapt the products to the specific markets of the individual countries
		Anxiety and a sense of insecurity in the future	People feel more uncertain about their position and their powers. We are not working effectively all the time	A little worried that work could be relocated to cheaper locations
		At first there was a fear for our jobs	On a wider scale (across the entire company), the situation is still fairly scattered, and nobody seems to be sure about anything	
		We are stuck in a rut and the overall picture is unclear.		

Anger	Anger. People don't appreciate each other between different departments	Are we equal? I sometimes feel that we Finns are being herded towards the German model like cattle	35% felt slightly, somewhat, significantly, or extremely angry
	Why do the krauts have the most power?	The flow of information is definitely not working properly. Communication is the worst area of the new company	6% felt significantly or extremely angry
	Will the wolf eat Little Red Riding Hood?	The values don't show anywhere	Work healthcare has gone downhill!!!!
	This has created chaos since we lack clear ownership roles and many important functions have "disappeared" from us and thus reduced our ability to have any influence and get information at the right time	At times, only negativity. Redundancies in departments suffering from perpetual understaffing. A system conversion with far too little preparation time and no consideration of the German market and its peculiarities. One cannot help the feeling that German employees are not taken seriously	I feel anger because sometimes I do not feel that the values given to the employees are being lived up to by the management. Even some managers of other departments are not living it
	Since the takeover by the Alpha Group, I cannot remember anything positive that I can be proud of!	At times it is annoying, not knowing who you should listen to: your own supervisor or a German person	Anger, because we do not really move forward at the construction sites and I sometimes get the impression that we are not pulling in the same direction
	I am not sure whether the values are actually being implemented and lived up to. There are examples that contradict this, already after a short time		
	Irrelevant for employees. Is not lived up to. No fairness—unequal treatment!		
Sadness	But after the last "round of dismissals" I was really speechless	Loss of identity	Not included
	Today I'm thinking that it actually was clear from the beginning that this could not proceed without losses. Beta has lost a part of its identity		
	I thought that the story of Alpha Finland will gradually end		
	Rewarding and encouragement will end completely		
Jealousy	Was Beta bought with the employees' operating profit bonus money?	It sometimes feels that Alpha taps are left in second place. Other than that, I have no complaints	Not included
	An unequal atmosphere	How much more money the Beta people make	

(*continued*)

Table 2.3 (continued)

Valence	*Emotion*[a]	*Quotes 2015*	*Quotes 2016*	*Percentages and elaboration 2018*
Mixed	Hope	Nevertheless, a small something called "hope" took hold of me. Slowly I am gaining confidence in the Alpha Group and I am praying that this will stay that way for a long time	We have a long way to go still, until all divisions/employees are integrated, so there is still a lot of potential	92% felt slightly, somewhat, significantly, or extremely hopeful
		Hopefully, the matrix and the values will take hold in the near future, and the old boy network will hopefully be broken up	Positive and expectant; the Germans are ambitious and competent, and also interested in other things than just earning more money themselves!	51% felt significantly or extremely hopeful
		I still believe in success, as long as people believe in it and have a proper setting and tools	Still expectant; it seems that we are still laying the foundation, and the topping-out ceremony is somewhere ahead	However, I hope that the investment has been planned for the long term, and it will still take some time until the two very different mentalities have fully found each other
		Hopefully, the product portfolio will actually become smaller in the future after the integration phase expansion and hopefully company-level decisions can be made as before, quickly and consistently	It's great that Alpha Group now has more muscle for the fight. On the other hand, the Group is facing enormous challenges in creating the new portfolio and organizing itself internally. Alpha should stop the trend of reducing turnover	Hopeful because Alpha Group has every chance of becoming a key player in the sanitation industry. Especially with the arrival of certain people, new ideas have come, along with the desire to do something really good
		Mainly positive thoughts, in daily work there are, however, ambiguities and different ways of doing things; it will get better in time, it's probably normal	Many misunderstandings between people. It seems that each brand staff still lives in its own world and doesn't show any effort. From the other side, I still believe that one day two different camps will start to work and live as one body and will create a big synergy. It's very big and the main task for the top-management people	There is definitely still some progress to be made. I am confident that we can get there
		I hope that people remember that everything depends on good cooperation and understanding and that they will try to work together in accordance with the values, helping each other		

[a]The emotions reflect Lazarus' (1993) categorization

positive perceptions about the company and the value renewal process, they increased unity and cooperation, and they encouraged the practical application of the values. Similarly, the values themselves triggered happiness, as they coincided with the employees' personal values and gave the company direction and motivation. The integration period triggered happiness due to the similarities perceived between Alpha and Beta, and the acquisition itself was experienced as a sign of strength and development. The atmosphere in the integrated company was considered positive.

> *The observation that we all, sometimes even unwittingly, have similar principles and values, was very constructive. In such a community it is easier to head in one direction—towards our common goal.*
> *(Survey respondent, 2015)*

> *Very positive! Remains a work in progress and all parties are continuing to communicate in order to form a harmonious entirety.*
> *(Survey respondent, 2016)*

Relief was felt when Alpha Group showed it cared for the employees, for example through inviting them to the workshops. Relief refers to perceived difficulties changing for the better (Lazarus 1993). The acquisition created confidence in the future and the integration restored feelings of job security. Some Alpha employees also felt relieved that they were employed by the acquiring organization during the deal, whereas some Beta members felt relieved to be out of the capital investor's hands.

> *Relief: It had been known for quite some time that [Beta] was up for sale. For a company like [Alpha], this takeover would only have made sense if one would intensively continue to use the products, know-how, and, above all, the market importance of [Beta] for oneself, which would include the continued existence of the production facilities and the brand name.*
> *(Survey respondent, 2015)*

Pride was triggered by the perceived good values and of belonging to a company with good values. Pride is born through taking credit for perceived accomplishments (Lazarus 1993). Alpha employees also took pride in being the buyer. In addition, the integration was seen as an accomplishment in terms of building a stronger company.

Makes me proud to work at a company that values honesty and fairness! It's good that we have outspoken values in the company.
(Survey respondent, 2015)

Hope, the fear of the worst but hoping for better (Lazarus 1993), also emerged very strongly and was the only mixed emotional state found at Alpha Group. Hope was triggered by seeing the potential the deal and the new values created, but at the same time observing that a long road would have to be travelled to achieve these. Employees were expectant and optimistic regarding the future, despite ongoing problems.

If the very top of the executive level gives an example of living up to these values, then the values and their claims become valid. In the interests of the [Alpha Group] and for the future of the company, I hope that these workshops will be carried out regularly in the future.
(Survey respondent, 2015)

There are differences between the German regions, and also with Finland. A different mindset and mentality. The merging process will continue to be a slow process. [—] There is still a lot of potential. I hope we will get more support, including staff, in Germany, and have our proposals taken into consideration.
(Survey respondent, 2016)

4.1.2 Negative Emotions

Anxiety was the most common negative emotion and it reflects facing an uncertain threat (Lazarus 1993). A key trigger was the integration with an unknown partner, where the possibility of resource reallocations created job insecurity. The employees also felt uncertainty when the integration process seemed slow and clouded the future of the company. Employees felt like their concerns had not been adequately heard and perceived the two companies as still separate; cooperation problems and quality issues persisted, and work overload increased stress.

I am afraid that due to control and the fear of failure, we will go years back in time, as responsibilities and decision-making, which were supposed to be brought closer to the field, have been taken further away.
(Survey respondent, 2015)

> *Confused—we are now in a situation where the honeymoon is over, and the daily toil has begun. I feel that pigeonholes and bunkers are now starting to appear as people are trying to determine their positions in the new organization.*
> *(Survey respondent, 2016)*

Anger also arose, reflecting perceived demeaning offences (Lazarus 1993). Some employees felt that the value workshops were badly organized as they took place immediately following layoffs and they did not offer any practical benefit. These employees perceived the value workshops as the company claiming the employees did not currently have such values. In addition, the lack of progress, particularly in working according to the values, created anger. Particularly the experience of inequality created anger. Similarly, employees saw consistent issues that were not solved by the integration.

> *It is an insult to the employees since it is subliminally being suggested that no "values" exist with the employees at [Beta]. The communicated values are self-evident "virtues" in daily working life and have therefore always been in existence!*
> *(Survey respondent, 2015)*

In addition, some sadness and jealousy emerged, reflecting perceived losses and favouritism, respectively (Lazarus 1993). *Sadness* was triggered by the loss of some colleagues due to layoffs and due to a perceived loss of pre-acquisition identity. Alpha members who perceived that Beta was gaining more control over the company, which was considered unfair, felt *jealous*.

4.1.3 Variation over Time

Overall, in 2015 (2016) 46% (38%) of all emotional comments reflected happiness, 11% (5%) relief, and 3% (2%) pride, the total of all positive emotion-laden comments being 60% (45%). Hope, the mixed emotion, represented 6% (19%) of the comments. In contrast, 24% (20%) represented anxiety, 8% (16%) anger, 1% (0%) sadness and 1% (0%) jealousy, the negative emotions thus totalling 34% (36%). In 2018, employees were asked if they felt happiness, relief, pride, anxiety, anger, or hope *not at all*, *slightly*, *somewhat*, *significantly*, or *extremely*. Overall, 90% (40%) of the respondents felt slightly, somewhat, significantly, or extremely (significantly or extremely) happy, 76% (29%) felt relieved, 90% (45%) proud, 54% (11%) anxious, 35% (6%) angry, and 92% (51%) felt hopeful. Altogether, 85% of the respondents reported to have experienced at least some positive emotions, 45% negative emotions and 92% mixed emotions. Figures 2.1, 2.2, and 2.3 illustrate the key findings from the different datasets.

Because the data-collection methods varied between each time point, it is impossible to make trustworthy cross-analyses. Particularly the framing of the question in 2018 increased the ease and therefore likely increased the occurrence of reporting emotions. However, the findings indicate changes in both emotion triggers and emotion intensity at different times following acquisition. Moreover, the 2018 data was collected shortly after four years had passed since the deal, meaning that this dataset reflects a return to business as usual rather than the integration period.

Between 2015 and 2016, when the change was fastest, the relative amount of anger compared to other emotions rose slightly. Similarly, negative emotion triggers rose in number between 2015 and 2016, while the number of positive emotion triggers decreased. At the same time, the focus of hope shifted from wishing for the enactment of the new values towards hoping for increased clarity in daily work. Also, in 2018, many

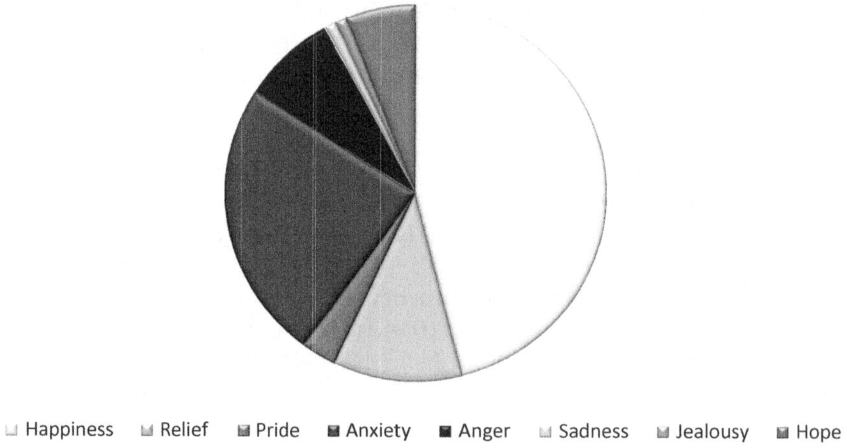

Fig. 2.1 Alpha Group emotions in 2015

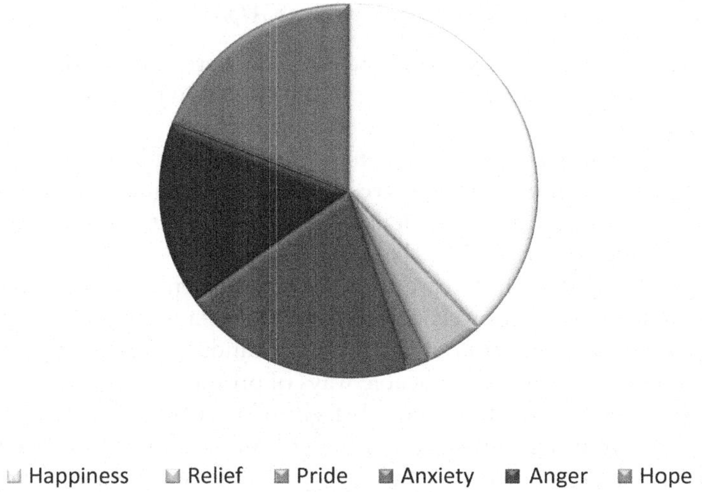

Fig. 2.2 Alpha Group emotions in 2016

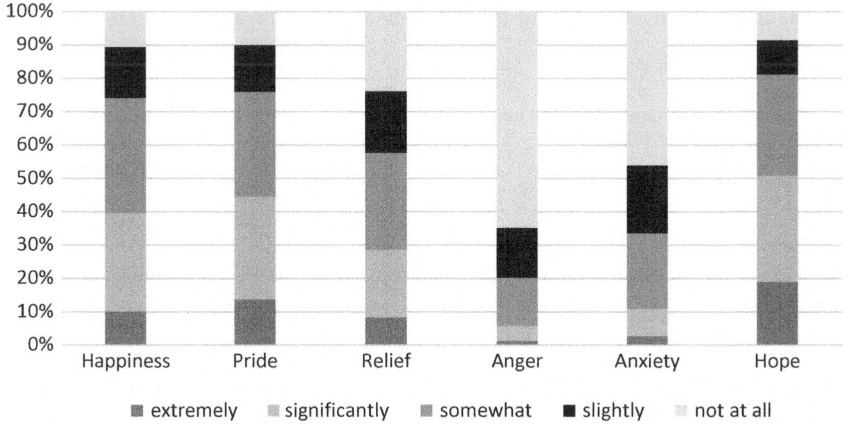

Fig. 2.3 Alpha Group emotions in 2018

more negative emotions were reported. However, it must be noted that in 2018 many more emotions in general were reported, likely due to the ease of responding to the statistical rather than to the open-ended questions. Nevertheless, positive emotions remained the most commonly reported throughout the datasets.

4.2 *Positive Change at Alpha Group*

The merger integration approach at Alpha Group was designed to avoid the all too common *us* versus *them* attitude known in the acquisition literature through increasing employee engagement and commitment. Arguably, Alpha Group was able to strengthen employee identification with the joint company and thus create unity. Illustrating the Alpha Group integration through the steps defined in Table 2.1, it becomes clear that positive change was central (Table 2.4).

Through engaging in research cooperation centring on employee emotions, Alpha Group showed interest in understanding how employees experience post-acquisition change. Understanding the current situation is a crucial step in finding applicable ways of promoting positive emotions. For this purpose, the employee satisfaction surveys asking employees to detail their emotions and concerns helped Alpha Group to identify both the negative aspects to correct and the positive ones to highlight. Similarly, the value workshops showed employees that the company was willing to engage everyone from the CEO to the line workers in the integration,

Table 2.4 Positive post-acquisition change at Alpha Group

Positive integration steps	*Alpha Group*
Detect and understand employee emotions in order to encourage positivity	1. Research cooperation centring on emotions 2. Employee survey to discover emotions 3. Value workshops to encourage positivity
Communicate the positive aspects of integration, creating a sense of excitement and readiness	1. Benefits from continuity, growth and internationalization 2. Excitement and readiness through engaging in value work
Form a compelling vision of the future of the integrated company	1. Joint values guiding work
Respond to employees' emotions in ways that encourage commitment to the integrated company	1. Value workshops 2. Increased communication based on research findings 3. Variety of communication means
Strengthen the achieved integration through encouraging employees to identify with the new organization	1. Value workshops 2. Promoting the new company name 3. Adopting the values in the long-term vision

creating a sense of appreciation. Based on employee perceptions and Alpha Group's reasoning for the deal, the benefits of continuity, growth and internationalization became the central message to emphasize the positive aspects of integration. This allowed employees to become excited about a new brighter future that the companies could build together. Readiness and excitement about change were boosted in the value workshops, where each employee could engage with the change effort on a very personal level, discussing how they could help unification through adopting the new values in their daily work.

The new values acted as the base for a compelling new vision; a joint unified company acting upon mutually agreed principles of good work. The new values, thanks to the value workshops, were seen as guiding work. The workshops also responded to employee concerns in encouraging commitment and engagement. Alpha Group also responded to employee concerns through increasing communication based on the feedback from the surveys and through adopting more varied communication channels in order to reach employees on a daily basis. For example, the new values were brought up in every employee meeting, appeared on notice boards and became the topic of recurrent comic strips in the company magazine. Finally, the value workshops were an endeavour at strengthening the new joint identity of Alpha Group. Similarly, Alpha Group eagerly promoted the use of the new company name, wishing to end the use of the old Alpha and Beta company names. Furthermore, the new company values were not forgotten once integration was over, but lived on as the basis of Alpha Group's identity, solidifying change.

> *The most important thing is to understand the people and speak with them, and to be open. It is communication—I cannot think of anything that would be more important.*
> *(Integration Manager, interview)*

These steps that were taken seem to prove that management today, and particularly successful change management, includes an emotional element (cf. Karp 2004). If positive is understood as goal-congruent and pleasing, creating a mutual goal (i.e. a future vision) is crucial in creating positivity regarding change. Only through establishing a mutually accepted goal can employees experience change as affirmative and, therefore, as positive (cf. Avey et al. 2008).

When you don't have one hundred per cent trust and things are not talked about with their proper names, our greatest risk is that we will make completely wrong decisions, when we believe what they say, and cannot read between the lines regarding what they actually meant.
(Vice President, Product Management, interview)

Even at work, we tend to see the negative more often than the positive. This highlights the necessity of boosting positive triggers so that employees can perceive the positive aspects of change, even if change creates some uncertainty (cf. Cameron 2008). Creating positivity through offering employees positive triggers such as a mutual goal is important due to the broadening effect of positive emotions compared to the fight-or-flight reactions caused by many negative emotions (cf. Fredrickson 2001).

I think this must, you must wait. I think I feel like Alpha Group but I'm … I think, what I say is, wait two or three years. Then, we will knit together. I think it's the same in Alpha. The people are thinking we are the best. And Beta thinks we are the best. [—] And they must learn to speak together. Look for the mistakes and then … do away with them.
(Internal Services Manager, Union Representative, interview)

Positive emotions also feed into a positive climate (Bar-tal et al. 2007), which eases post-acquisition change (cf. Fischer and Manstead 2008; Vacharkulksemsuk et al. 2010). At Alpha Group, a positive climate was supported through taking employees' emotional needs into consideration and encouraging positive emotions (cf. Ozcelik et al. 2008).

People appreciate that they are now much more involved than before.
(Vice President, Sales in German-Speaking Areas, interview)

Although Alpha Group employees experienced both positive and negative emotions—as is expected –, the change climate remained positive due to the willingness to consider emotions and place an emphasis on joint trust and security (cf. Bar-tal et al. 2007). The positive climate, in turn, had the expected result of increasing positive emotions, such as happiness and pride, as well as encouraging positive organizational behaviour, such as adopting the new values in daily work (cf. Bar-tal et al. 2007). In addition, it seemed that employees experiencing positive emotions were more receptive to and engaged in change, highlighting the importance of creating positivity rather than simply alleviating negativity.

4.3 *Managing Positive Change at Alpha Group*

At Alpha Group, it seems that managing successful change indeed highlights commitment-building and change receptiveness (cf. Caldwell 2003). Through interactive communication means, particularly the value workshops, Alpha Group managers were able to increase employee contentment and show encouragement, boosting the emergent positive climate (cf. Maimone and Sinclair 2010). The value workshops were an example of an active initiative to encourage the emergence of a positive work climate, whereas the extensive employee satisfaction surveys showed an interest in employees' emotional needs (cf. Ozcelik et al. 2008).

> *By presence. I was practically, I would say, six days a week for several months out of house. Just being present in the countries, discussing things with people, explaining the strategy, explaining Alpha Group.*
> *(Vice President, Sales Central and Eastern Europe, interview)*

Alpha Group managers were also able to engage employees in change through communicating its importance. The future success of the joint company was a powerful image to which the employees were able to commit (cf. Whetten and Cameron 2011). The managers were aware that the emotions and attitudes they portrayed had an influence on the employees (cf. Hatfield et al. 1994).

> *Yeah it's, well takeovers are emotional. [—] And then if you cannot express your emotions, they might come over the wrong way. And the recipients get it the wrong way. And then, it leads to misunderstandings. And I had a couple of these run-ins.*
> *(Vice President, Purchasing and Logistics, interview)*

In some cases, this increased the managers' emotional toll when they experienced the need to mask their true emotions for the benefit of the employees. While the wish to do so shows emotional intelligence, in effect, managers were engaging in emotion work (cf. Hochschild 2012).

> *That is my problem with this, that I know just as well as my subordinates do that our resources and competences that we have in the organization are not sufficient. And the conflict here is that I am never allowed to admit that. [—] It is especially difficult not to be able to say to your subordinate that you are absolutely right.*
> *(CFO, interview)*

Nevertheless, managerial example proved a powerful emotion trigger, somewhat surprisingly particularly in terms of negative emotions. Employees highlighted that when managers were seen to violate the new values, it undermined the entire change process.

> *Only, the department managers should also observe this! Because some department managers are only busy with embracing coffee machines, or with getting orders for their second or third company!!!! And that is at our expense, and without any counteroffers etc.!!!*
> *(Survey respondent, 2015)*

The clearest example of facilitation (Cameron and Green 2012) was in organizing and moderating the value workshops. In these workshops, designated facilitators promoted discussion and mutual understanding in an effort to encourage change-congruent behaviour.

> *The value workshops were important for the integration of Alpha and Beta. They influence the daily work, in our interaction with customers, colleagues and superiors.*
> *(Survey respondent, 2015)*

> *The value workshop was a very rewarding experience. It produced a lot of discussion about values and provided many tools for the future.*
> *(Survey respondent, 2015)*

As the workshops had the clearly defined objective of introducing the values to the employees and helping them to adopt the values in their daily work, the employees were able to easily engage in the change. The values also embodied the vision for the company's future, solidifying the change effort and, in effect, switching ownership to the employees (cf. Whetten and Cameron 2011). Adopting the new values as part of daily work enabled employees to commit to the change and thereby increase its durability (cf. Armenakis et al. 1999). As value-congruent work practices became routine, they institutionalized the change (cf. Kotter 1995).

5 Conclusion

This chapter set out to explore (1) *What constitutes positive change management following a cross-border acquisition*? and (2) *How can positive change management ease post-acquisition integration*? To answer these questions, this chapter adopted a POS lens, highlighting the positive emotional aspects of acquisitions. In the literature, positive emotions were discovered to be of crucial importance following acquisitions (e.g. Birkinshaw et al. 2000; Kusstatscher and Cooper 2005; Raitis et al. 2017). Such positivity stems from pleasant sensations (Gordon 1987) linked to personal objectives (Lazarus 1991). In harnessing such positivity during change, it is therefore necessary to ensure the affirmative nature of the change process (cf. Avey et al. 2008). Based on the literature, five steps of positive change management following acquisitions were identified: detecting and understanding employee emotions, creating a sense of excitement and readiness, forming a compelling vision of the future, responding to employees' emotions and encouraging employees to identify with the new organization.

The illustrative case showed how—possibly unconsciously—managers had followed these steps during the post-acquisition integration at Alpha Group. Positive change management eased post-acquisition change by engaging employees to take ownership of the change. This reveals that the influence of emotions on change processes can be great. Emotions arise in change situations that employees consider to be personally relevant. Such emotions can be positive or negative, depending on how goal-congruent or pleasing employees evaluate the change to be. Through active emotion management, companies can offer employees a myriad of positive emotion triggers and thereby encourage the emergence of positive emotions. Because positive emotions are particularly beneficial for change (e.g. Birkinshaw et al. 2000; Fredrickson 2001; Fischer and Manstead 2008; Vacharkulksemsuk et al. 2010), boosting positivity is likely to ease change much more than through merely addressing negative emotions. Boosting positive emotions also creates a positive change climate where change will occur more swiftly and more smoothly. A positive change climate, in turn, can act as a further positive emotion trigger.

Based on the findings, managers should not only seek to address employee concerns, but they should also actively promote the emergence of positive emotions during post-acquisition change. Furthermore, positive emotions triggered through engaging employees in the change, for example through interactive workshops, seems most beneficial in terms of creating change ownership and motivating employees to drive and institutionalize the change. To achieve these objectives, it seems beneficial to employ change management with high emotional intelligence, as this will ease the task of detecting and responding to employee emotions. Change management should also be able to clearly and convincingly communicate the positive aspects of the change to the employees in order to create excitement. Forming a compelling vision of the future of the integrated company is therefore essential. In addition, change management must be able to respond to employee emotions in ways that encourage commitment to the integrated company and motivate employees to work towards the vision. Finally, being able to engage employees in carrying out and maintaining the change will ease the institutionalization of the change and, at the same time, encourage identification with the post-acquisition organization.

References

Armenakis, A., Harris, S., & Feild, H. (1999). Making change permanent: A model for institutionalizing change interventions. In W. Pasmore & R. Woodman (Eds.), *Research in organizational change and development* (Vol. 12, pp. 97–128). Bingley: Emerald.

Ashkanasy, N. M. (2003). Emotions in organizations: A multi-level perspective. *Research in Multi-Level Issues, 2*, 9–54. https://doi.org/10.1016/S1475-9144(03)02002-2.

Ashkanasy, N. M., & Daus, C. S. (2002). Emotion in the workplace: The new challenge for managers. *Academy of Management Executive, 16*(1), 76–86.

Avey, J. B., Wernsing, T. S., & Luthans, F. (2008). Can positive employees help positive organizational change? Impact of psychological capital and emotions on relevant attitudes and behaviors. *Journal of Applied Behavioral Science, 44*(1), 48–70. https://doi.org/10.1177/0021886307311470.

Bar-tal, D., Halperin, E., & DeRivera, J. (2007). Collective emotions in conflict situations: Societal implications. *Journal of Societal Issues, 63*(2), 441–460.

Birkinshaw, J., Bresman, H., & Håkanson, L. (2000). Managing the post-acquisition integration process: How the human integration and task integration processes interact to foster value creation. *Journal of Management Studies, 37*(3), 395–425. https://doi.org/10.1111/1467-6486.00186.

Bono, J. E., & Ilies, R. (2006). Charisma, positive emotions and mood contagion. *Leadership Quarterly, 17*(4), 317–334. https://doi.org/10.1016/j.leaqua.2006.04.008.

Caldwell, R. (2003). Change leaders and change managers: Different or complementary? *Leadership & Organization Development Journal, 24*(5/6), 285–293.

Cameron, K. (2008). Paradox in positive organizational change. *Journal of Applied Behavioral Science, 44*(1), 7–24. https://doi.org/10.1177/0021886308314703.

Cameron, K. (2012). *Positive leadership: Strategies for extraordinary performance* (2nd ed.). San Francisco, CA: Berrett-Koehler.

Cameron, K. (2017). Cross-cultural research and positive organizational scholarship. *Cross Cultural and Strategic Management, 24*(1), 13–22. https://doi.org/10.1108/CCSM-02-2016-0021.

Cameron, E., & Green, M. (2012). *Making sense of change management: A complete guide to the models, tools and techniques of organizational change*. London: Kogan Page.

Cameron, K., Dutton, J., & Quinn, R. (2003). Foundations of positive organizational scholarship. In K. Cameron, J. Dutton, & R. Quinn (Eds.), *Positive organizational scholarship: Foundations of a new discipline* (pp. 3–13). San Francisco, CA: Berrett-Koehler.

Cartwright, S., & Cooper, C. L. (1993). The role of culture compatibility in successful organizational marriage. *Academy of Management Perspectives, 7*(2), 57–70. https://doi.org/10.5465/AME.1993.9411302324.

Cartwright, S., & Cooper, C. L. (1995). Organizational marriage: "Hard" versus "soft" issues? *Personnel Review, 24*(3), 32–42. https://doi.org/10.1108/00483489510089632.

DeRivera, J., & Páez, D. (2007). Emotional climate, human security, and cultures of peace. *Journal of Social Issues, 63*(2), 233–253.

Dhingra, R., & Punia, B. K. (2016). Relational analysis of emotional intelligence and change management: A suggestive model for enriching change management skills. *Vision, 20*(4), 312–322. https://doi.org/10.1177/0972262916668726.

Fink, G., & Yolles, M. (2015). Collective emotion regulation in an organisation: A plural agency with cognition and affect. *Journal of Organizational Change Management, 28*(5), 832–871. https://doi.org/10.1108/JOCM-09-2014-0179.

Fischer, A. H., & Manstead, A. S. R. (2008). Social functions of emotion. In M. Lewis, J. Haviland-Jones, & L. F. Barrett (Eds.), *Handbook of emotions* (3rd ed., pp. 456–468). New York: The Guilford Press.

Fletcher, M., & Plakoyiannaki, E. (2011). Case selection in international business: Key issues and common misconceptions. In R. Piekkari & C. Welch (Eds.), *Rethinking the case study in international business and management research* (pp. 171–191). Cheltenham: Edward Elgar.

Flyvbjerg, B. (2001). *Making social science matter: Why social inquiry fails and how it can succeed again*. Cambridge: Cambridge University Press.

Fredrickson, B. L. (2001). The role of positive emotions in positive psychology. *American Psychologist, 56*(3), 218–226. https://doi.org/10.1037/0003-066X.56.3.218.

Fredrickson, B. L. (2013). Positive emotions broaden and build. In P. Devine & A. Plant (Eds.), *Advances in experimental social psychology* (pp. 1–53). Burlington: Academic. https://doi.org/10.1016/B978-0-12-407236-7.00001-2.

Gardner, L., & Stough, C. (2002). Examining the relationship between leadership and emotional intelligence in senior level managers. *Leadership & Organization Development Journal, 23*(2), 68–78. https://doi.org/10.1108/01437730210419l9.

George, J. M. (2000). Emotions and leadership: The role of emotional intelligence. *Human Relations, 53*(8), 1027–1055. https://doi.org/10.1177/0018726700538001.

Goleman, D. (1998). What makes a leader. *Harvard Business Review, 76*(6), 93–102. https://doi.org/10.13445/j.cnki.t.e.r.2014.03.007.

Gooty, J., Connelly, S., Griffith, J., & Gupta, A. (2010). Leadership, affect and emotions: A state of the science review. *Leadership Quarterly, 21*(6), 979–1004. https://doi.org/10.1016/j.leaqua.2010.10.005.

Gordon, R. (1987). *The structure of emotions: Investigations in cognitive philosophy.* Cambridge: Cambridge University Press.

Graebner, M. E., Heimeriks, K., Huy, Q., & Vaara, E. (2017). The process of postmerger integration: A review and agenda for future research. *Academy of Management Annals, 11*(1), 1–32. https://doi.org/10.5465/annals.2014.0078.

Harikkala-Laihinen, R., Hassett, M., Raitis, J. and Nummela, N. (2018), "Dialogue as a source of positive emotions during cross-border post-acquisition socio-cultural integration", *Cross Cultural & Strategic Management, 25*(1), pp. 183–208. https://doi.org/10.1108/CCSM-09-2016-0163.

Haspeslagh, P., & Jemison, D. (1991). *Managing acquisitions: Creating value through corporate renewal.* New York: The Free Press.

Hatfield, E., Cacioppo, J., & Rapson, R. (1994). Primitive emotional contagion. In M. Clark (Ed.), *Emotion and social behavior: The review of personality and social psychology* (14th ed., pp. 151–177). London: SAGE.

Hochschild, A. (2012). *Managed heart: Commercialization of human feeling* (3rd ed.). Berkeley: University of California Press.

Johnson, S. K. (2008). I second that emotion: Effects of emotional contagion and affect at work on leader and follower outcomes. *Leadership Quarterly, 19*(1), 1–19. https://doi.org/10.1016/j.leaqua.2007.12.001.

Karp, T. (2004). Learning the steps of the dance of change: Improving change capabilities by integrating futures studies and positive organisational scholarship. *Foresight, 6*(6), 349–355. https://doi.org/10.1108/14636680410569920.

Kotter, J. (1995). Leading change: Why transformation efforts fail the promise of the governed corporation. *Harvard Business Review, 73*(2), 59–67.

Kusstatscher, V. (2006). Cultivating positive emotions in mergers and acquisitions. *Advances in Mergers and Acquisitions, 5*, 91–103.

Kusstatscher, V., & Cooper, C. (2005). *Managing emotions in mergers and acquisitions.* Cheltenham: Edward Elgar.

Lazarus, R. (1991). *Emotion and adaptation.* New York: Oxford University Press.

Lazarus, R. (1993). From psychological stress to the emotions: A history of changing outlooks. *Annual Review of Psychology, 44*, 1–21. https://doi.org/10.1146/annurev.psych.44.1.1.

Luthans, F., & Youssef, C. (2007). Emerging positive organizational behavior. *Journal of Management, 33*(3), 321–349. https://doi.org/10.4135/9781446212752.

Maimone, F., & Sinclair, M. (2010). Affective climate, organizational creativity, and knowledge creation: Case study of an automotive company. In W. Zerbe, C. Härtel, & N. Ashkanasy (Eds.), *Emotions and organizational dynamism: Research on emotion in organizations* (Vol. 6, pp. 309–332). Bingley: Emerald. https://doi.org/10.1108/S1746-9791(2010)0000006016.

Marks, M. L., & Mirvis, P. H. (2011). A framework for the human resources role in managing culture in mergers and acquisitions. *Human Resource Management, 50*(6), 859–877. https://doi.org/10.1002/hrm.20445.

Mayer, J., & Caruso, D. (2002). The effective leader: Understanding and applying emotional intelligence. *Ivey Business Journal, 67*(2), 1–5.

Menges, J. I., & Kilduff, M. (2015). Group emotions: Cutting the gordian knots concerning terms, levels of analysis, and processes. *Academy of Management Annals, 9*(1), 845–928. https://doi.org/10.1080/19416520.2015.1033148.

Momeni, N. (2009). The relation between managers' emotional intelligence and the organizational climate they create. *Public Personnel Management, 38*(2), 35–48.

Newcombe, M. J., & Ashkanasy, N. M. (2002). The role of affect and affective congruence in perceptions of leaders: An experimental study. *Leadership Quarterly, 13*(5), 601–614. https://doi.org/10.1016/S1048-9843(02)00146-7.

Ovans, A. (2015, April 28). How emotional intelligence became a key leadership skill. *Harvard Business Review Online.* Retrieved August 3, 2020, from https://hbr.org/2015/04/how-emotional-intelligence-became-a-key-leadership-skill.

Ozcelik, H., Langton, N., & Aldrich, H. (2008). Doing well and doing good: The relationship between leadership practices. *Journal of Managerial Psychology, 23*(2), 186–203. https://doi.org/10.1108/02683940810850817.

Patton, M. Q. (2015). *Qualitative research & evaluation methods: Integrating theory and practice* (4th ed.). London: SAGE.

Raitis, J., Harikkala-Laihinen, R., Hassett, M., & Nummela, N. (2017). Finding positivity during a major organizational change: In search of triggers of employees' positive perceptions and feelings. In W. Zerbe, C. Härtel, N. Ashkanasy, & L. Petitta (Eds.), *Emotions and identity: Research on emotion in organizations* (Vol. 13, pp. 3–16). https://doi.org/10.1108/S1746-979120170000013001.

Raitis, J., Harikkala-Laihinen, R., Hassett, M., & Nummela, N. (2018). *Socio-cultural integration in mergers and acquisitions: The Nordic approach*. Cham: Palgrave Pivot.

Roberts, L. M. (2006). Shifting the lens on organizational life: The added value of positive scholarship. *Academy of Management Review, 31*(2), 292–305.

Ruddin, L. P. (2006). You can generalize stupid! Social scientists, bent Flyvbjerg, and case study methodology. *Qualitative Inquiry, 12*(4), 797–812. https://doi.org/10.1177/1077800406288622.

Russell, J. (2008). Promoting subjective well-being at work. *Journal of Carer Assessment, 16*(1), 117–131. https://doi.org/10.1177/1069072707308142.

Salovey, P., & Mayer, J. D. (1990). Emotional intelligence and its relationship to other intelligences. *Cognition and Personality, 9*(3), 185–211. https://doi.org/10.1037/0022-3514.50.2.421.

Sarala, R. M., Vaara, E., & Junni, P. (2019). Beyond merger syndrome and cultural differences: New avenues for research on the "human side" of global mergers and acquisitions (M&As). *Journal of World Business, 54*(4), 307–321. https://doi.org/10.1016/j.jwb.2017.10.001.

Stahl, G. K., & Tung, R. L. (2015). Towards a more balanced treatment of culture in international business studies: The need for positive cross-cultural scholarship. *Journal of International Business Studies, 46*(4), 391–414. https://doi.org/10.1057/jibs.2014.68.

Stahl, G. K., Tung, R. L., Kostova, T., & Zellmer-Bruhn, M. (2016). Widening the lens: Rethinking distance, diversity, and foreignness in international business research through positive organizational scholarship. *Journal of International Business Studies, 47*(6), 621–630. https://doi.org/10.1057/jibs.2016.28.

Stake, R. (1995). *The art of case study research*. Thousand Oaks, CA: SAGE.

Vacharkulksemsuk, T., Sekerka, L. E., & Fredrickson, B. L. (2010). Establishing a positive emotional climate to create 21st-century organizational change. In N. M. Ashkanasy, C. P. M. Wilderom, & M. F. Peterson (Eds.), *The handbook of organizational culture and climate* (pp. 101–118). Thousand Oaks, CA: SAGE.

Waddell, D., & Sohal, A. S. (1998). Resistance: A constructive tool for change management. *Management Decision, 36*(8), 543–548. https://doi.org/10.1108/00251749810232628.

Whetten, D., & Cameron, K. (2011). *Developing management skills* (8th ed.). Boston: Prentice Hall.

CHAPTER 3

Finding Unity in a Friendly Takeover

Abstract This chapter centres on finding unity when the *us* versus *them* thinking that is common in acquisitions is heightened. This setting often triggers negative protectionist attitudes in the target company employees. However, with careful emotion management, the integration process can become swifter and smoother. This chapter introduces a German–Finnish acquisition completed in early 2017. The findings stem from interviews, memo-like diaries and an employee satisfaction survey collected between 2017 and 2018. The findings indicate that understanding how group-shared and group-based emotions emerge in organizations based on either co-presence or identification can increase companies' ability to influence employee emotions. Moreover, offering the employees positive emotion triggers through a positive emotional climate at work can greatly enhance unity during integration.

Keywords Group emotions • Merger syndrome • Unity

1 Introduction

Human-centric acquisition research to date is built on three interconnected streams (Sarala et al. 2019). The first highlights the merger syndrome and overcoming negative emotions (Cartwright and Cooper 1993;

R. Harikkala-Laihinen, *Managing Emotions in Organizations*,
https://doi.org/10.1007/978-3-030-60567-4_3

e.g. Marks and Mirvis 1997; Sinkovics et al. 2011). The second focuses on the influence of cultural differences (Morosini et al. 1998; Teerikangas and Very 2006; Björkman et al. 2007). The third centres on managerial concerns and practice, including HRM (Sarala et al. 2019). Within these streams, differences between the acquisition parties are often highlighted. Particularly cultural distance (Slangen 2006; e.g. Chakrabarti et al. 2009; Rottig 2017; Xie et al. 2017) and how to manage under the condition of differences (e.g. Kedia et al. 2011; Weber and Drori 2011; Teerikangas 2012; Lin et al. 2015; Brueller et al. 2018) have puzzled scholars and practitioners alike.

However, a key objective of post-acquisition integration is the creation of unity. Thus, calls for a more balanced treatment of culture and increasing positive foci in acquisition research have arisen (e.g. Cameron 2008; Stahl and Tung 2015; Stahl et al. 2016). Particularly the emergence of positive emotions (e.g. Kusstatscher 2006; Harikkala-Laihinen 2019) and positive outcomes, such as identification with the post-acquisition organization (e.g. Kusstatscher and Cooper 2005; Raitis et al. 2017), can increase understanding in acquisition research. The previous negative bias of acquisition research (e.g. Graebner et al. 2017; Sarala et al. 2019) has left room for increasing research on the positive side of cross-cultural research, such as acquisitions (e.g. Cameron 2017).

This chapter focuses on *how to build unity between* us *and* them *following acquisitions.* In effect, the purpose of this chapter is to reveal how negative group emotions and the merger syndrome can be overcome to build a harmonious coexistence. Particularly, this chapter explores the creation and influence of a positive climate on post-acquisition change. While positive climates are known to ease change, the literature on how to create and manage them is scarce (Canning and Found 2015; Dixon et al. 2016). Particularly how the surrounding climate influences individual emotions (Helpap and Bekmeier-Feuerhahn 2016) and how the climate can predict collective behaviour (cf. Schultz et al. 2017) necessitate further research. Similarly, the interconnections between individual emotions and organizational outcomes continue to be puzzling. Thus, exploring emotions at different levels offers a fruitful avenue for research (Menges and Kilduff 2015; Ashkanasy et al. 2017; Parke and Seo 2017).

2 Group Emotions and Unity

2.1 Group-Based and Group-Shared Emotions

Although emotions are inherently subjective, individual emotions may converge to become group phenomena. Group emotions arise when a number of individuals respond similarly to the same event (Kemper 2002). Membership in a particular social group increases the likelihood of group emotions, because members are more likely to react similarly to external stimuli, thus giving rise to similar emotional responses to events that the members perceive as relevant for the social group (Goldenberg et al. 2014).

Group emotions most often represent perceptions that arise either in or from group membership. *Group-shared* emotions arise in groups due to co-presence. An often-cited example of group-shared emotions is the atmosphere of excitement experienced at a rock concert or a sporting event. In contrast, *group-based* emotions are born from group membership. For example, national pride arises from groups (Menges and Kilduff 2015).

In organizations, different groups emerge at different organizational levels. Whereas individual emotions often reflect *me*, what will happen to the individual employee, group emotions may reflect several different groups, what will happen to *us*. First, employees experience group membership with their immediate colleagues, possibly called a team. A single employee may be a part of several such groups within an organization, based on the organizational structure and the employee's personal preference (Harikkala-Laihinen 2019). Nevertheless, at a team level, employees consider their immediate colleagues, mirroring and reflecting others' responses to find synchrony and harmony within the group (Harikkala-Laihinen 2019; cf. Lanzetta and Englis 1989; Hatfield et al. 1994).

Following acquisitions, two additional group levels arise: the pre- and post-acquisition organizational levels. At the pre-acquisition organizational level, group emotions reflect the collective *us* opposed to the collective *them*. Employees are likely to identify with the accustomed pre-acquisition organization, particularly triggering group-based emotions. At the post-acquisition level, the joint company is central. The key perspective becomes the new *we* (Harikkala-Laihinen 2019). Nevertheless, during integration, the *us* versus *them* attitudes, in effect, the in-group–out-group bias, often triggers problems due to the protectionist attitudes adopted by employees in fear of excessive change (Menges et al. 2015).

2.2 *The Merger Syndrome*

The *merger syndrome* is a fear-the-worst, fight-or-flight response to acquisitions. It stems from the *us* versus *them* attitude and causes major stress in the involved employees, complicating integration (e.g. Marks and Mirvis 1997; Kusstatscher and Cooper 2005; Sinkovics et al. 2011). The merger syndrome can be understood when acquisitions are seen as adaptation processes rather than as singular events (Cartwright and Cooper 1995). This perspective takes the sociocultural challenges (e.g. Datta 1991; Birkinshaw et al. 2000; Marks and Mirvis 2011; Raitis et al. 2018) of integration into account.

Often, the merger syndrome is a question of acculturation. Acculturation refers to the meeting, clashing and eventual adaptation of the two previously separate cultures of the acquisition partners (Nahavandi and Malekzadeh 1988; Rottig et al. 2013). In acquisitions, the result of successful acculturation is the formation of a unified culture from the previously separate sets of organizational beliefs and values (Larsson and Lubatkin 2001). However, the change necessary to achieve acculturation, in effect the experience of conflict and adaptation, often lead to change resistance. The merger syndrome represents the worst-case scenario of this resistance (cf. Marks and Mirvis 1997; Kusstatscher and Cooper 2005; Sinkovics et al. 2011).

To be successful, acculturation necessitates social controls. In effect, this means socializing the affected employees, for example via training, social gatherings, or information exchange (Larsson and Lubatkin 2001). This is akin to creating a new organizational culture. Thus, problems mainly arise when the norms and values of the acquisition partners are different (Stahl et al. 2013). The possible culture clashes that complicate integration and hinder acculturation manifest as stereotyping, highlighting differences and belittling the acquisition partner's culture (Marks and Mirvis 2011). When the merger syndrome emerges, finding unity becomes increasingly difficult.

2.3 *Finding Unity Between* Us *and* Them

The *Oxford English Dictionary* defines *unity* as the state of forming a complete and harmonious whole. There are several potential hurdles to successful unity-building following acquisitions. For example, perceived inequality in decision-making power is often experienced as unfair and lessens the willingness to learn about the acquisition partner (Schweiger et al. 1993). These tensions are heightened if employees perceive high disparity (Björkman et al. 2007), a wide power distance (Stahl and Sitkin 2005), or decreasing autonomy (Larsson and Lubatkin 2001). In contrast, when cooperation is perceived as leading to just, mutually beneficial outcomes, employees are more likely to work together (Melkonian et al. 2011). Similarly, how the process is managed (Kavanagh and Ashkanasy 2006), how fast the integration is implemented (Recardo and Tortehi 2015; Angwin et al. 2016), how great the perceived extent of the cultural change is (Kavanagh and Ashkanasy 2006) and how much distance is between the acquisition partner's management styles, languages, practices etc. (Risberg 2001) will inevitably influence the involved employees' attitudes towards integration.

The key issue with finding unity is that whatever the extent of the change is, employees are likely to react to it as if they were undergoing a redesign merger (Cartwright and Cooper 1993; cf. Teerikangas and Irrmann 2016; Harikkala-Laihinen 2019). Change resistance stems from an aversion to the unknown (Dhingra and Punia 2016). However, uncertainty is not always dominant. If the involved employees perceive positive outcomes, such as personal and organizational development opportunities, their attitudes shift towards motivation (Teerikangas 2012). A key way in which to encourage post-acquisition unity is to create a positive change climate (cf. Fischer and Manstead 2008). As stated in Chap. 1, an organization's emotional climate refers to the felt working atmosphere (DeRivera and Páez 2007) and reflects the visible part of the organization's culture (Momeni 2009). A positive emotional climate refers to an atmosphere where all emotions are allowed and which pays attention to the employees' emotional needs and well-being (Harikkala-Laihinen 2019).

In an emotional climate, negative and positive features correlate with negative and positive emotions and beliefs. Thus, a stressful atmosphere will likely trigger anxiety, whereas a peaceful environment will more likely trigger a sense of security or hope. Moreover, a negative climate is likely to trigger negative behaviours, whereas a positive climate supports positive behaviours (Bar-tal et al. 2007). Therefore, the emotional climate surrounding post-acquisition change can predict collective emotions and behaviour. Because group-based and group-shared emotions (i.e. collective emotions) suggest an underlying similarity in perceptions and beliefs, they also influence collective behaviour. For example, collective anger often leads to behaviour designed to remove a perceived obstacle, whereas collective hope is likely to encourage group activity in support of the future (DeRivera and Páez 2007).

Just as several organizational groups can emerge and trigger collective emotions at different organizational levels, separate emotional climates can appear in a myriad of organizational groups (Ruiz 2007; Härtel and Liu 2012). A group's emotional climate is more lasting and objective than the group emotions, which shape and obey the climate (cf. Tran 1998; DeRivera and Páez 2007; Momeni 2009). Such group climates feed on the social sharing of emotional experiences, which over time establish a set of attitudes and behaviours that are common in the group. What kinds of behaviours the group climate supports depends on the valence of the emotions the climate is built on as well as on the shape of the social engagement within the group (Härtel and Liu 2012). This is why some groups are more ego-focused, placing the needs of the self above the needs of others, whereas other groups are more other-focused, placing someone else at the core (Markus and Kitayama 1991). Socially disengaged, ego-focused groups could experience, for example, climates of unhappiness (negative valence) or pride (positive valence), whereas the socially engaged, other-focused groups could be characterized by jealousy (negative) or commiseration (positive) (Härtel and Liu 2012).

The key ways for building a positive climate centre on offering the employees positive emotion triggers (Harikkala-Laihinen 2019). A positive climate can be encouraged through increasing employee contentment, ensuring an efficient and ergonomic physical working space, and maintaining a desired leadership style (Maimone and Sinclair 2010). In addition, sensitivity to emotional needs, explicit positive encouragement from superiors, as well as active, engaging initiatives to create a pleasing atmosphere at work are likely to inspire a positive emotional climate (Ozcelik et al. 2008).

3 Method

3.1 *The Gamma–Delta Acquisition*[1]

German Gamma bought Finnish Delta in early 2017. Gamma was a large international group with operations that were complementary to Delta's.

[1] The data for this chapter has previously been discussed in Harikkala-Laihinen, R. (2019) *The power of positivity: How employee emotions and interaction can benefit cross-border acquisitions.* Turku: University of Turku.

This chapter is written from Delta's point of view, thus representing the acquired company. Delta was a small industrial company, employing 77 workers. It was struggling with profitability and had suffered from occasional layoffs for years. Nevertheless, Delta's quality standards were high, and their product range was competitive. Delta's brand was well-known and trusted, and sales were strong in Europe, the Middle East and India. Thus, Gamma saw the acquisition as an opportunity to widen its product portfolio, whereas Delta wished for increased resources and competitiveness.

As Gamma was an established large player in the field, had global operations and saw Delta's product lines as complementary to their own, having previously been a customer of Delta, it chose a traditional, rather slow integration approach. Although Gamma led the integration, the slow approach meant that for the first six months after the deal, very little change was visible for Delta employees. For example, the Gamma and Delta brand names remained separate. Still, quality standards and daily processes such as reporting systems, financial management systems and management structures needed unification. Gamma mainly enforced task-related integration (cf. Birkinshaw et al. 2000), seeking mainly operational synergies. The integration strategy resembles symbiosis (cf. Haspeslagh and Jemison 1991), as Gamma chose strategic integration, leaving Delta with very little strategic independence or operational decision-making power, even though Delta's operations continued much as usual.

3.2 Data Collection and Analysis

Data collection occurred at Delta between May 2017 and March 2018. The core of the data consists of 26 interviews (Table 3.1), 17 conducted in summer 2017, and nine in spring 2018. The interviewees represented a cross-section of organizational functions and hierarchical levels, and included one representative of Gamma—the Integration Manager and new Deputy Managing Director of Delta. The interviews lasted between 30 and 60 minutes, totalling 865 (2017) and 456 (2018) minutes. All but two interviews were conducted in the Delta offices, and all but two interviews were conducted in Finnish. Due to overseas locations, two interviews were conducted via Skype, and due to differences in mother tongues, two interviews were conducted in English. The interviews were

Table 3.1 Delta interviews

Interviewee title	*Function*	*Duration 2017*	*Duration 2018*
Managing Director	Top management	58 min	58 min
Deputy MD, Integration Manager	Top management	63 min	52 min
Supply Chain Director	Production	48 min	29 min
Chief Financial Officer, Personnel Director	Finance	62 min	57 min
Country Manager	Sales	53 min	51 min
Manager	Sales	41 min	–
Customer Service Coordinator	Customer Service	50 min	57 min
Senior Purchaser	Purchasing	58 min	–
Purchaser	Purchasing	44 min	–
Logistics and Quality Manager	Logistics	62 min	–
R&D and Training Manager	Technology	62 min	49 min
Manufacturing Supervisor	Production	41 min	–
Assembly Supervisor	Production	46 min	49 min
Employee	Production	38 min	–
Employee	Production	55 min	–
Employee	Production	62 min	54 min
Employee	Warehouse	59 min	–

transcribed to ease analysis, which occurred through qualitative coding in QSR NVivo software. The coding themes arose from both theoretical insights as well as from the data itself. The key themes were the deal, communication, emotions, emotional climate, management and future.

In addition, Delta employees were invited to write a memo-like diary on 3-to-5 consecutive days asking about their daily rating of the working atmosphere at Delta, the emotions they had felt or they had detected at Delta and their thoughts on how to improve the working atmosphere at Delta. In 2017, the diary was open to the 17 interviewees, and ten respondents made 44 entries. In 2018, every employee at Delta was invited to join, but only six respondents participated with altogether 21 entries. All diary entries were written in Finnish. The employees' numeric evaluations of the atmosphere at Delta were analysed quantitatively for a quick overview, but the core of the data was analysed thematically in order to discover common emotion triggers at Delta. These were further categorized into positive and negative aspects. As the diaries were relatively brief, the diary data had a supportive role.

Finally, Delta employees were invited to answer open-ended questions regarding their perceptions about the acquisition, communication, working atmosphere and management in an employee satisfaction survey in October 2017. The questions reflected the key findings from the 2017 interviews. Altogether 56 employees responded to the survey, representing some 59% of the Delta employees, at that time totalling 95. The survey data was also analysed based on qualitative themes. As the survey questions reflected the key themes found in the interview data, the responses were used to further inform the interview findings. To ensure complete anonymity, all quotations used are made fully unrecognizable.

4 Finding Unity Between Gamma and Delta

4.1 Emotions at Delta

Despite Gamma's slow and task-focused integration approach, Delta employees experienced adaptation to a new normal, reflecting some level of acculturation and organizational socialization (cf. Larsson and Lubatkin 2001). At the same time, the employees appreciated the Delta name and brand intactness following the acquisition. This highlights the unity dilemma; whatever the extent of the change is, employees are likely to react to it as if they were undergoing a redesign merger (Cartwright and Cooper 1993; cf. Teerikangas and Irrmann 2016; Harikkala-Laihinen 2019). Indeed, the employees seemed keenly aware of the power disparity (cf. Stahl and Sitkin 2005; Björkman et al. 2007) and decreased autonomy (cf. Larsson and Lubatkin 2001), creating negativity towards integration. Nevertheless, the emotions at Delta varied greatly, reflecting both positive and negative experiences (Table 3.2).

On the positive side, Gamma was perceived as an interesting company. The development opportunities the deal brought, the complementary nature of the product offerings and the family-owned structure of Gamma made Delta employees more comfortable.

> *Now we have more resources backing us so that we can develop production. I have been saying for years that we need certain things, more investments and improved efficiency.*
>
> *(Manufacturing Supervisor, 2017)*

Table 3.2 Emotions at Delta

Core themes	*Representative quotations*
Happiness over development	"Investments are positive for the whole company, and the new recruitment. They build faith in continuity" "There have been positive things like investments and that gives faith in the future" "I really feel like I'm part of this. And they make me feel very welcome" "Peace and a happy feeling—they hopefully will carry us for a long time" "It is always positive when things come to a conclusion" "They are nice people and it is easy to get along with them" "We do have a good group spirit; we can all laugh at the same things"
Relief over continuity	"The times before the deal were … I often felt like something must happen" "I was relieved. I saw it as positive for Delta and Delta's employees" "I am now a bit relieved that the beginning of the year is over, but for the whole of the beginning of the year I have felt annoyed, really, because there was too much work" "To get some new kick into this—for that reason I thought it was positive. I've been thinking that this can't get much worse" "They don't have our main products; that makes me feel easier"
Pride over Delta practices	"In the end Delta is an old company, so being Finnish and where this all begun, somehow you want to hold onto that" "They want to learn more about our products, and we can help them" "Our way of doing things is definitely better" "In a way change triggers anger because I think common sense should be allowed. They are making my work more difficult" "Speaking straight, the change was ridiculous"
Anxiety over the future	"If you don't know what is going on, you feel a little insecure about everything" "People are quite irritated and tired; you can tell that the positivity that has always been a great resource for us has diminished significantly" "There are things that aren't under our control and that seems difficult" "Compared to our resources, too much is demanded from us. We have too many projects" "There is frustration going around, there has been a lot of bungling things up, start this, stop this, change this, repair this, repair that, the bungling up is disconcerting" "With the people that I'm working with it's, I think there is quite a lot of tension"

Besides investments, Gamma was perceived to offer increased internal sales opportunities and wider networks. Gamma colleagues were welcomed and interaction with them was enjoyed. Similarly, Gamma's previous acquisitions had not led to major layoffs, which reassured Delta employees.

When the new owners were here to introduce themselves, it gave me a good feeling. And that they had production all over Europe, they are not concentrated in just one country.
(Production employee, 2017)

The bi-annual staff meetings at Delta were much appreciated and the announcement of the deal on one such event was considered well organized and positive. An issue of the in-house magazine was dedicated to introducing the acquisition partners to each other. Overall, Delta employees were happy and relieved about the continuity and faith in the future the deal brought. They felt proud about the accustomed best practices at Delta, wishing to carry them over to Gamma.

On the negative side, Delta employees were used to a very flat organization, whereas Gamma had a clear hierarchy, which it forced upon Delta. The wider networks and hierarchy brought along some confusion regarding responsibilities. At the same time, Delta's future within Gamma seemed foggy, triggering uncertainty and lowering motivation.

People are tired and frustrated. I hear deep sighs and frustrated comments.
(Diarist, 2017)

However, due to Gamma's slow integration approach, very little change was visible to some employees in 2017. Change was even hoped for, as the employees perceived change as a signal that integration was moving forward. Nevertheless, particularly in the 2018 interviews, the perception that growth had brought challenges was common. Changing financial reporting systems and pending plans to renew the enterprise resource planning system caused stress and anxiety. Increasing workloads were taking a toll on the employees.

We have no choice; things just have to move forward, so we just grit our teeth.
(Chief Financial Officer, Personnel Director, 2018)

Overall, more active communication from Gamma was hoped for, while bottom-up messages from Delta were often perceived as having disappeared. Internal sales were not picking up and Delta was hoping that Gamma would take a more active role in promotion. This was a key anger trigger, as Gamma was seen to accuse Delta of its declining bottom line, of which Gamma's new practices of internal sales and reporting were the cause. Delta employees also took offence over Gamma's desire to change Delta's best practices. What were particularly negative were the perceptions that Gamma was dispelling Delta's identity, increasing the *us* versus *them* attitudes of the merger syndrome.

4.2 Group Emotions and the Merger Syndrome at Delta

At Delta, group emotions largely reflected group membership rather than co-presence. In effect, it seems that at Delta, group-based emotions were stronger than group-shared emotions were (cf. Menges and Kilduff 2015). While employees were concerned about their personal future in the organization, the future of their immediate work group and Delta as a whole was considered more important. Initial emotions reflected the employee's team or function at Delta (e.g. will manufacturing be discontinued, how can the warehouse cope with change, what will the customer managers do in the future?), whereas emotions regarding the organization as a whole reached a higher level of abstraction (e.g. what will Gamma's strategy for Delta be in the future?). Particularly the pride over Delta's best practices, the anger at Gamma's disrupting them and the happiness over continuity reflect group emotions born out of membership at Delta. However, the group emotions seemed to centre around *us*, the pre-acquisition company. Gamma was seen as *them*, "the other party". In effect, the post-acquisition joint *we* did not emerge.

> *It's more, understanding and, sometimes if I say yes, it's not a yes on the other side. It's as simple as that. [—] If they always say "them", then it's more challenging to grow together. I always pay very much attention to that.*
> *(Deputy Managing Director, Integration Manager, 2018)*

Delta employees expressed the feeling that Gamma had not embraced them as a part of the company. For example, Delta employees felt like their ideas were not heard, that Gamma did not really understand Delta's practices and that switching to some of Gamma's practices actually meant a deterioration. The employees wished Gamma would ask about the relevant functions when planning changes in order to make sure the strategy was actually sensible and implementable. Delta employees felt like Gamma was blaming everything on Delta, even though Delta had no power.

> *Well, it doesn't feel all that nice, when … when things happen that you don't see as very sensible.*
> *(Chief Financial Officer, Personnel Director, 2018)*

The employees saw Delta as valuable and identified strongly with the pre-acquisition organization, which caused them to fear that over time, Delta would disappear completely into Gamma. For example, Delta employees preferred communication from old Delta managers rather than from Gamma. In addition, communication about strategic decisions made at Gamma was seen as lacking at Delta. Overall, communication between different organizational functions and levels was seen as sub-optimal, which caused annoyance and rumour-mongering.

> *One [challenge] is making out the future. What we are going to continue, what is left here and what might move somewhere else. And what it is sensible to do here.*
> *(Supply Chain Director, 2017)*

At Delta, the key stressors that encouraged the merger syndrome were the insecurity felt over the future, the unsustainably high workloads, the loss of decision-making power, the confusion over responsibilities and the lack of positive signals regarding the deal. Arguably, these issues were difficult to adapt to (cf. Cartwright and Cooper 1995) and reflect a clash between the involved organizations (cf. Nahavandi and Malekzadeh 1988; Rottig et al. 2013). At Delta, it was clear that social gatherings (such as the Christmas party) and information exchange (such as the staff meetings) created positivity towards the deal, reflecting socialization (cf. Larsson and Lubatkin 2001). However, because the norms and practices of Gamma—possibly due to its sheer size—were different from what was accustomed to at Delta, problems arose (cf. Stahl et al. 2013). Employees highlighted differences between Gamma and Delta practices and somewhat belittled Gamma (cf. Marks and Mirvis 2011), stating, "Our way of doing things is definitely better."

Overall, Delta employees experienced that negative emotions spread very fast, particularly between immediate colleagues. Nevertheless, although during the time of data collection the Delta employees did start to experience fight-or-flight responses that are common for the merger syndrome (cf. Marks and Mirvis 1997; Sinkovics et al. 2011), they were also experiencing hope, signalling that the merger syndrome had not yet taken hold. The hope for a better future, the hope for realized synergies and the hope for improved operations were the foundation upon which to build unity.

4.3 Finding Unity at Delta

Delta employees commended managers for their ability to calm down anxious employees. Nevertheless, the employees felt that if management showed more positivity, the changes would be easier to digest and more motivating. Particularly team-level communication was called for, as employees felt too nervous to ask questions when the entire company was present at the staff meetings. A key to building unity and alleviating anxiety, according to Delta employees, would have been a clearer vision for the future. Similarly, cooperation and interaction between units was seen as a good way to increase unity. In addition, creating a sense of ownership through participation would have motivated the employees.

Despite some negative perspectives, Delta employees felt that the company had always enjoyed a positive climate. This was seen to help in the post-acquisition period. Employees generally enjoyed coming to work, and appreciated joking and laughing together during breaks. The low employee turnover rate and friendly atmosphere reflected the positive climate. Delta as a company was seen to treat employees well, which in turn motivated employees. The positive climate also contributed to performance. Employees tried to be proactive and go beyond their mandate whenever they saw something in need of doing. They cared about their colleagues and helped others whenever necessary. They felt free to ask for help and were always offered constructive advice. They also felt that the positive climate increased their pace and, thereby, their performance.

> *It [a positive emotional climate] is—in terms of working atmosphere—it is essential. That it is nice to come [to work] and work goes well. That there is more than just completing tasks at your post, that you have breaks and what not. It is essential. If we didn't have that, this would be quite a gloomy toil.*
> *(Assembly Supervisor, 2017)*

Nevertheless, the acquisition had caused many rumours, raising anxiety. This started to seep into the emotional climate. Uneven workloads were seen as unfair and acquisition-related stress caused tempers to shorten. The foggy future meant employees did not see that they could affect their own future in any way, which felt disheartening. By the time the second wave of interviews were held in 2018, the employees experienced the atmosphere at Delta as more critical and achievement-centred than before. Increasing pressure meant that employees started to worry about future coping.

> *People are rather irritable and tired, and you can see that the positivity I always thought was our strength has decreased considerably.*
> *(Country Manager, 2018)*

However, the employees still felt positive towards the successful completion of some integration projects. Despite the deterioration, the accustomed helpfulness and friendliness remained topmost in terms of the atmosphere. The positive climate extended to interaction with Gamma colleagues, and the continuity and slowly appearing investments into Delta raised spirits.

> *In the end I feel better than last autumn, and we have now had many positive things like investments and such, so of course they build faith in the future.*
> *(Supply Chain Manager, 2018)*

The employees' perceptions reveal that Delta was in fact suffering from many of the hurdles introduced above. The employees reported feelings of inequality and loss of power (cf. Schweiger et al. 1993; Stahl and Sitkin 2005), decreasing autonomy (cf. Larsson and Lubatkin 2001) and high disparity (cf. Björkman et al. 2007). While Delta managers were commended for their efforts (cf. Kavanagh and Ashkanasy 2006), the speed of the integration seemed too slow at first, and too fast in the end (cf. Recardo and Tortehi 2015; Angwin et al. 2016), complicating the process. Similarly, although little cultural change was planned, its perceived extent (cf. Kavanagh and Ashkanasy 2006) was much greater, as wide differences were seen, for example, in management styles and practices (cf. Risberg 2001). In contrast, the employees' wish for a clarified strategy and future vision reflects the necessity of perceiving cooperation as a way towards mutually beneficial outcomes (cf. Melkonian et al. 2011).

Indeed, even though Gamma's integration plan did not include full amalgamation, Delta employees felt almost as if they were undergoing a redesign merger (cf. Cartwright and Cooper 1993). Particularly the unknown future created change resistance (cf. Dhingra and Punia 2016). Still, the development opportunities the deal afforded were seen as positive, increasing motivation somewhat (cf. Teerikangas 2012). Particularly the employees' appreciation of Delta managers' concern for their emotional well-being reflected a positive climate even following the acquisition (cf. Harikkala-Laihinen 2019).

At Delta, the valence of the climate did result in the relevant behaviour (cf. Bar-tal et al. 2007). The positive climate encouraged employees to be proactive and helpful, whereas the deteriorating climate correlated with increased stress and anxiety. Thus, the surrounding climate did also predict collective emotions and behaviour (cf. DeRivera and Páez 2007). The group-based emotions reflecting Delta's identity drove the employees to resist changes they saw as threatening to the norm at Delta (cf. Menges and Kilduff 2015), but collective hope emerged based on the synergy potential seen in the deal (cf. DeRivera and Páez 2007).

Nevertheless, several somewhat separate climates were also visible at Delta. While the overarching emotional climate at the company did appear somewhat unified, it reflected the pre-acquisition company. Thus, in Gamma's new hierarchy, Delta itself formed one sub-climate. In addition, the different functions at Delta had slightly varying experiences (cf. Härtel and Liu 2012). On the factory floor where the changes were the slowest to appear, the climate did not reflect the acquisition to a great extent, but showed the everyday concerns over, for example, machinery quality. However, at the same time, the financial team was undergoing major stress due to switching to new reporting systems, increasing stress and negativity towards Gamma. Similarly, the sales representatives were working extremely hard at switching clients to new, local Gamma suppliers. It seemed that particularly the negative features of the climate seemed group-specific, whereas the positive features reflected Delta's working atmosphere as a whole. Similarly, the negativity in the groups seemed more other-focused and socially engaged, reflecting, for example, jealousy over Gamma's power, whereas the positive, more organization-centric emotions were somewhat ego-focused, reflecting pride over Delta.

The positive connotation of Delta membership, while motivating in itself, did not encourage employees to identify with Gamma. In addition, because Delta employees did not experience active engagement in the change, positive emotions about integrating with Gamma still mainly reflected Delta concerns. Whereas the investments and increased resources created positive feelings towards Gamma, a compelling future vision did not emerge. The chosen integration approach, while aiming at keeping Delta employees comfortable, may in fact have given Delta employees a false sense of stability, expecting no changes. However, as synergy-seeking acquisitions most often lead to some level of integration, change was inevitable. Thus, when change emerged, it triggered negative emotions compared to the expected stability.

4.4 Increasing Unity Between Gamma and Delta

As positivity seemed strongly related to continuity and opportunity, highlighting these would arguably have created more unity between Gamma and Delta. In contrast, as negativity reflected perceived uncertainty and inequality, tackling these through clear strategic directions and increased communication may have helped alleviate the negative emotions. Because the post-acquisition period was characterized by different groups, paying attention to varied experiences may also have helped. The immediate work group, often called a team, was the first sounding board for the emotions triggered by the deal and subsequent changes. At this level, emotions were also highly contagious, with most functional units reporting very similar experiences. The teams which experienced most change also experienced most stress and anxiety, as may be expected.

However, the crucial difference lies between the pre- and post-acquisition organizational level. Identification with the pre-acquisition organization (i.e. Delta) led to heightened *us* versus *them* attitudes, as it created a sense of belonging to Delta rather than to Gamma. This identification triggered emotions reflecting the future of the in-group rather than of the post-acquisition organization as a whole. The post-acquisition organization, while triggering both positive emotions regarding Gamma as the buyer and negative emotions regarding the changes brought on by the deal, did not induce identity-related positivity (i.e. a sense of belonging to Gamma). This is a crucial difference when considering unity with the acquiring organization.

Engaging Delta employees with Gamma, for example, through interaction, may have helped build unity between the companies. Because the general purpose of interaction is to influence others (Buller and Burgoon 1996), organizational imprinting can also occur through interaction (cf. Kopelman et al. 2006). Human responsiveness to social contexts (Fiske and Taylor 2013) means that manipulating organizational climates to appear more positive can increase actual, experienced positivity (cf. Hatfield et al. 1994). To succeed, this necessitates the creation of togetherness and cooperation, which can help overcome the *us* versus *them* thinking. This can also help employees feel a sense of ownership of the integration process, motivating them to engage in change-congruent behaviour (Harikkala-Laihinen 2019). Whereas togetherness and cooperation did occur at Delta, much of it only reflected the pre-acquisition organization and did not extend to Gamma.

Interaction is also uniquely effective in creating positivity regarding change. Whereas traditional top-down communication is essential in keeping employees informed and alleviating worries, such information sharing alone will likely neutralize employee reactions rather than increase positivity (Harikkala-Laihinen 2019). However, even if formal company-initiated interaction is successful in increasing positivity, emotions—including negative emotions—are equally likely to spread through coffee table discussions (cf. Marmenout 2011). This highlights the importance of a positive climate. Nevertheless, for the positive climate to encourage change-congruent behaviour and identification with the new organization (cf. Fischer and Manstead 2008), a mutual goal must be perceptible to the employees (cf. Sekerka and Fredrickson 2008).

Within the positive climate, it is essential to highlight that all emotions—not just positive ones—are allowed and all employee concerns matter (cf. Bar-tal et al. 2007; Ozcelik et al. 2008). Still, a positive climate supports the emergence of positive emotions (Bar-tal et al. 2007), which can ease integration (Birkinshaw et al. 2000). Managers' efforts in building commitment and change receptiveness (cf. Caldwell 2003) may therefore be essential. Showing employees what is exciting about the change (Karp 2004) can encourage them to see the change as affirmative (cf. Whetten and Cameron 2011). This is why emotional intelligence (e.g. Goleman 1998; Gardner and Stough 2002; Ovans 2015) may be crucial for integration management.

5 Conclusion

This chapter has explored *how to build unity between* us *and* them *following acquisitions*. To achieve this objective, the chapter has highlighted how emotions are linked to change-congruent attitudes among employees. Particularly positive emotions regarding the post-acquisition organization seem crucial in engaging employees in change efforts. In contrast, positive emotions reflecting the pre-acquisition organization may in fact hinder integration, as they increase employee identification with the old company. Nevertheless, acquisitions do trigger uncertainty, and negative emotions often follow. Thus, to build positivity, the negative emotions must be detected by management, heard, managed and dissolved.

The emotional climate seems particularly effective in boosting morale following acquisitions. A positive climate can enhance positive emotions and positive behaviour, easing post-acquisition change. However, should the climate deteriorate, problems arise and accumulate. It seems that individual and collective emotions affect organizational outcomes through their behavioural effect. Positive emotions are likely to lead to positive behaviour, whereas negative emotions are likely to lead to negative behaviour. Seeing as a positive climate supports the emergence of positive emotions, the emotional climate surrounding change is essential. However, for the positive climate to be effective in motivating change-congruent behaviour and building unity, the employees must be able to work towards a mutual goal. Working towards a joint objective increases identification with the post-acquisition organization.

The climate surrounding the change is not merely a context—the walls around change—but is an active part of the change. This climate predates and outlives the change, but can greatly influence the change atmosphere following acquisitions. Thus, knowing the key elements of the involved organizations' emotional climates can help in finding and building unity between them. Because the climate influences employee experiences and behaviour, understanding and being able to influence the climate can help direct employee efforts during change periods. Making sure the emotional climate is positive may be a key way in which to manage collective emotions during change.

Creating a positive emotional climate seems to depend somewhat on managerial action. While an emotional climate is a product of collective emotions, through offering positive emotion triggers supporting feelings of ownership, happiness, or pride, managers can help shape the surrounding climate. In addition, managers should be open to hearing employee concerns and highlight the positive aspects of change, including establishing a positive future vision. This may necessitate high emotional intelligence. Because a positive climate refers to acceptance and well-being rather than solely positive emotions, it can also help employees cope with the negative emotions that often emerge following acquisitions. Furthermore, positivity can increase employee engagement and motivation.

References

Angwin, D. N., Mellahi, K., Gomes, E., & Peter, E. (2016). How communication approaches impact mergers and acquisitions outcomes. *International Journal of Human Resource Management, 27*(20), 2370–2397. https://doi.org/10.1080/09585192.2014.985330.

Ashkanasy, N. M., Humphrey, R. H., & Huy, Q. N. (2017). Integrating emotions and affect in theories of management. *Academy of Management Review, 42*(2), 175–189.

Bar-tal, D., Halperin, E., & DeRivera, J. (2007). Collective emotions in conflict situations: Societal implications. *Journal of Societal Issues, 63*(2), 441–460.

Birkinshaw, J., Bresman, H., & Håkanson, L. (2000). Managing the post-acquisition integration process: How the human integration and task integration processes interact to foster value creation. *Journal of Management Studies, 37*(3), 395–425. https://doi.org/10.1111/1467-6486.00186.

Björkman, I., Stahl, G. K., & Vaara, E. (2007). Cultural differences and capability transfer in cross-border acquisitions: The mediating roles of capability complementarity, absorptive capacity, and social integration. *Journal of International Business Studies, 38*(4), 658–672. https://doi.org/10.1057/palgrave.jibs.8400287.

Brueller, N. N., Carmeli, A., & Markman, G. D. (2018). Linking merger and acquisition strategies to postmerger integration: A configurational perspective of human resource management. *Journal of Management, 44*(5), 1793–1818. https://doi.org/10.1177/0149206315626270.

Buller, D. B., & Burgoon, J. K. (1996). Interpersonal deception theory. *Communication Theory, 6*(3), 203–242. https://doi.org/10.1111/j.1468-2885.1996.tb00127.x.

Caldwell, R. (2003). Change leaders and change managers: Different or complementary? *Leadership & Organization Development Journal, 24*(5/6), 285–293. https://doi.org/10.1108/01437730310485806.

Cameron, K. (2008). Paradox in positive organizational change. *Journal of Applied Behavioral Science, 44*(1), 7–24. https://doi.org/10.1177/0021886308314703.

Cameron, K. (2017). Cross-cultural research and positive organizational scholarship. *Cross Cultural and Strategic Management, 24*(1), 13–22. https://doi.org/10.1108/CCSM-02-2016-0021.

Canning, J., & Found, P. A. (2015). The effect of resistance in organizational change programmes: A study of a lean transformation. *International Journal of Quality and Service Sciences, 7*(2/3), 274–295. https://doi.org/10.1108/IJQSS-02-2015-0018.

Cartwright, S., & Cooper, C. L. (1993). The role of culture compatibility in successful organizational marriage. *Academy of Management Perspectives, 7*(2), 57–70. https://doi.org/10.5465/AME.1993.9411302324.

Cartwright, S., & Cooper, C. L. (1995). Organizational marriage: "Hard" versus "soft" issues? *Personnel Review, 24*(3), 32–42. https://doi.org/10.1108/00483489510089632.

Chakrabarti, R., Gupta-Mukherjee, S., & Jayaraman, N. (2009). Mars–Venus marriages: Culture and cross-border M&A. *Journal of International Business Studies, 40*(2), 216–236. https://doi.org/10.1057/jibs.2008.58.

Datta, D. K. (1991). Organizational fit and acquisition performance: Effects of post-acquisition integration. *Strategic Management Journal, 12*(4), 281–297. https://doi.org/10.1002/smj.4250120404.

DeRivera, J., & Páez, D. (2007). Emotional climate, human security, and cultures of peace. *Journal of Social Issues, 63*(2), 233–253.

Dhingra, R., & Punia, B. K. (2016). Relational analysis of emotional intelligence and change management: A suggestive model for enriching change management skills. *Vision, 20*(4), 312–322. https://doi.org/10.1177/0972262916668726.

Dixon, M., Lee, S., & Ghaye, T. (2016). Strengths-based reflective practices for the management of change: Applications from sport and positive psychology. *Journal of Change Management, 16*(2), 142–157.

Fischer, A. H., & Manstead, A. S. R. (2008). Social functions of emotion. In M. Lewis, J. Haviland-Jones, & L. F. Barrett (Eds.), *Handbook of emotions* (3rd ed., pp. 456–468). New York: The Guilford Press.

Fiske, S., & Taylor, S. (2013). *Social cognition: From brains to culture* (2nd ed.). London: SAGE.

Gardner, L., & Stough, C. (2002). Examining the relationship between leadership and emotional intelligence in senior level managers. *Leadership & Organization Development Journal, 23*(2), 68–78. https://doi.org/10.1108/01437730210419l9.

Goldenberg, A., Saguy, T., & Halperin, E. (2014). How group-based emotions are shaped by collective emotions: Evidence for emotional transfer and emotional burden. *Journal of Personality and Social Psychology, 107*(4), 581–596. https://doi.org/10.1037/a0037462.

Goleman, D. (1998). What makes a leader. *Harvard Business Review, 76*(6), 93–102. https://doi.org/10.13445/j.cnki.t.e.r.2014.03.007.

Graebner, M. E., Heimeriks, K. H., Huy, Q. N., & Vaara, E. (2017). The process of postmerger integration: A review and agenda for future research. *Academy of Management Annals, 11*(1), 1–32. https://doi.org/10.5465/annals.2014.0078.

Harikkala-Laihinen, R. (2019). *The power of positivity: How employee emotions and interaction can benefit cross-border acquisitions.* Turku: University of Turku.

Härtel, C., & Liu, X.-Y. (2012). How emotional climate in teams affects workplace effectiveness in individualistic and collectivistic contexts. *Journal of Management & Organization, 18*(4), 573–585. https://doi.org/10.5172/jmo.2012.18.4.573.

Haspeslagh, P., & Jemison, D. (1991). *Managing acquisitions: Creating value through corporate renewal.* New York: The Free Press.

Hatfield, E., Cacioppo, J., & Rapson, R. (1994). Primitive emotional contagion. In M. Clark (Ed.), *Emotion and social behavior: The review of personality and social psychology* (14th ed., pp. 151–177). London: SAGE.

Helpap, S., & Bekmeier-Feuerhahn, S. (2016). Employees' emotions in change: Advancing the sensemaking approach. *Journal of Organizational Change Management, 29*(6), 903–916. https://doi.org/10.1108/JOCM-05-2016-0088.

Karp, T. (2004). Learning the steps of the dance of change: Improving change capabilities by integrating futures studies and positive organisational scholarship. *Foresight, 6*(6), 349–355. https://doi.org/10.1108/14636680410569920.

Kavanagh, M. H., & Ashkanasy, N. M. (2006). The impact of leadership and change management strategy on organizational culture and individual acceptance of change during a merger. *British Journal of Management, 17*(SUPPL. 1). https://doi.org/10.1111/j.1467-8551.2006.00480.x.

Kedia, S., Ravid, S. A., & Pons, V. (2011). When do vertical mergers create value? *Financial Management, 40*(4), 845–877. https://doi.org/10.1111/j.1755-053X.2011.01164.x.

Kemper, T. D. (2002). Predicting emotions in groups: Some lessons from September 11. *The Sociological Review, 50*(S2), 53–68.

Kopelman, S., Rosette, A. S., & Thompson, L. (2006). The three faces of eve: Strategic displays of positive, negative, and neutral emotions in negotiations. *Organizational Behavior and Human Decision Processes, 99*(1), 81–101. https://doi.org/10.1016/j.obhdp.2005.08.003.

Kusstatscher, V. (2006). Cultivating positive emotions in mergers and acquisitions. *Advances in Mergers and Acquisitions, 5*, 91–103.

Kusstatscher, V., & Cooper, C. (2005). *Managing emotions in mergers and acquisitions.* Cheltenham: Edward Elgar.

Lanzetta, J. T., & Englis, B. G. (1989). Expectations of cooperation and competition and their effects on observers' vicarious emotional responses. *Journal of Personality and Social Psychology, 56*(4), 543–554. https://doi.org/10.1037/0022-3514.56.4.543.

Larsson, R., & Lubatkin, M. (2001). Achieving acculturation in mergers and acquisitions: An international case survey. *Human Relations, 54*(12), 1573–1607. https://doi.org/10.1177/00187267015412002.

Lin, B. W., Chen, W. C., & Chu, P. Y. (2015). Mergers and acquisitions strategies for industry leaders, challengers, and niche players: Interaction effects of technology positioning and industrial environment. *IEEE Transactions on Engineering Management, 62*(1), 80–88. https://doi.org/10.1109/TEM.2014.2380822.

Maimone, F., & Sinclair, M. (2010). Affective climate, organizational creativity, and knowledge creation: Case study of an automotive company. In W. Zerbe, C. Härtel, & N. Ashkanasy (Eds.), *Emotions and organizational dynamism: Research on emotion in organizations* (Vol. 6, pp. 309–332). Bingley: Emerald. https://doi.org/10.1108/S1746-9791(2010)0000006016.

Marks, M. L., & Mirvis, P. H. (1997). Revisiting the merger syndrome: Crisis management. Part 2. *Mergers and Acquisitions, 31*(6), 21–27.

Marks, M. L., & Mirvis, P. H. (2011). A framework for the human resources role in managing culture in mergers and acquisitions. *Human Resource Management, 50*(6), 859–877. https://doi.org/10.1002/hrm.20445.

Markus, H. R., & Kitayama, S. (1991). Culture and the self: Implications for cognition, emotion, and motivation. *Psychological Review, 98*(2), 224–253. https://doi.org/10.1037/0033-295X.98.2.224.

Marmenout, K. (2011). Peer interaction in mergers: Evidence of collective rumination. *Human Resource Management, 50*(6), 783–808. https://doi.org/10.1002/hrm.20458.

Melkonian, T., Monin, P., & Noorderrhaven, N. (2011). Distributive justice, procedural justice, exemplarity, and employees' willingness to cooperate in M&A integration processes: An analysis of the air France–KLM merger. *Human Resource Management, 50*(6), 809–837.

Menges, J. I., & Kilduff, M. (2015). Group emotions: Cutting the gordian knots concerning terms, levels of analysis, and processes. *Academy of Management Annals, 9*(1), 845–928. https://doi.org/10.1080/19416520.2015.1033148.

Menges, J. I., Kilduff, M., Kern, S., & Bruch, H. (2015). The awestruck effect: Followers suppress emotion expression in response to charismatic but not individually considerate leadership. *The Leadership Quarterly, 26*(4), 626–640. https://doi.org/10.1016/j.leaqua.2015.06.002.

Momeni, N. (2009). The relation between managers' emotional intelligence and the organizational climate they create. *Public Personnel Management, 38*(2), 35–48.

Morosini, P., Shane, S., & Singh, H. (1998). National cultural distance and cross-border acquisition performance. *Journal of International and Intercultural Communication, 29*(1), 137–158.

Nahavandi, A., & Malekzadeh, A. R. (1988). Acculturation in mergers and acquisitions. *Academy of Management Review, 13*(1), 79–90. https://doi.org/10.5465/AMR.1988.4306790.

Ovans, A. (2015, April 28). How emotional intelligence became a key leadership skill. *Harvard Business Review Online*. Retrieved August 3, 2020, from https://hbr.org/2015/04/how-emotional-intelligence-became-a-key-leadership-skill.

Ozcelik, H., Langton, N., & Aldrich, H. (2008). Doing well and doing good: The relationship between leadership practices. *Journal of Managerial Psychology, 23*(2), 186–203. https://doi.org/10.1108/02683940810850817.

Parke, M. R., & Seo, M.-G. (2017). The role of affect climate in organizational effectiveness. *Academy of Management Review, 42*(2), 334–360.

Raitis, J., Harikkala-Laihinen, R., Hassett, M., & Nummela, N. (2017). Finding positivity during a major organizational change: In search of triggers of employees' positive perceptions and feelings. In W. Zerbe, C. Härtel, N. Ashkanasy, & L. Petitta (Eds.), *Emotions and identity: Research on emotion in organizations* (Vol. 13, pp. 3–16). https://doi.org/10.1108/S1746-979120170000013001.

Raitis, J., Harikkala-Laihinen, R., Hassett, M., & Nummela, N. (2018). *Socio-cultural integration in mergers and acquisitions: The Nordic approach.* Cham: Palgrave Pivot.

Recardo, R., & Tortehi, T. (2015). Strategic integration: How to realize the value of an acquisition. *Global Business and Organizational Excellence, 35*(1), 6–22.

Risberg, A. (2001). Employee experiences of acquisition processes. *Journal of World Business, 36*(1), 58–84.

Rottig, D. (2017). Meta-analyses of culture's consequences for acquisition performance: An examination of statistical artifacts, methodological moderators and the context of emerging markets. *International Journal of Emerging Markets, 12*(1), 8–37. https://doi.org/10.1108/IJoEM-01-2015-0003.

Rottig, D., Reus, T. H., & Tarba, S. (2013). The impact of culture on mergers and acquisitions: A third of a century of research. *Advances in Mergers and Acquisitions, 12*, 135–172. https://doi.org/10.1108/MRR-09-2015-0216.

Ruiz, J. (2007). Emotional climate in organizations: Applications in Latin American prisons. *Journal of Social Issues, 63*(2), 289–306.

Sarala, R. M., Vaara, E., & Junni, P. (2019). Beyond merger syndrome and cultural differences: New avenues for research on the "human side" of global mergers and acquisitions (M&As). *Journal of World Business, 54*(4), 307–321. https://doi.org/10.1016/j.jwb.2017.10.001.

Schultz, J. S., Sjøvold, E., & Andre, B. (2017). Can group climate explain innovative readiness for change? *Journal of Organizational Change Management, 30*(3), 440–452. https://doi.org/10.1108/JOCM-06-2016-0112.

Schweiger, D., Csiszar, E., & Napier, N. (1993). Implementing international mergers and acquisitions. *Human Resource Planning, 16*(1), 53–70.

Sekerka, L. E., & Fredrickson, B. L. (2008). Establishing positive emotional climates to advance organizational transformation. In N. Ashkanasy & C. Cooper (Eds.), *Research companion to emotion in organizations* (pp. 531–545). Cheltenham: Edward Elgar.

Sinkovics, R. R., Zagelmeyer, S., & Kusstatscher, V. (2011). Between merger and syndrome: The intermediary role of emotions in four cross-border M&As. *International Business Review, 20*(1), 27–47. https://doi.org/10.1016/j.ibusrev.2010.05.002.

Slangen, A. H. L. (2006). National cultural distance and initial foreign acquisition performance: The moderating effect of integration. *Journal of World Business, 41*(2), 161–170. https://doi.org/10.1016/j.jwb.2006.01.003.

Stahl, G. K., & Sitkin, S. (2005). Trust in mergers and acquisitions. In G. K. Stahl & M. Mendenhall (Eds.), *Mergers and acquisitions: Managing culture and human resources* (pp. 82–102). Stanford: Stanford Business Books.

Stahl, G. K., & Tung, R. L. (2015). Towards a more balanced treatment of culture in international business studies: The need for positive cross-cultural scholarship. *Journal of International Business Studies, 46*(4), 391–414. https://doi.org/10.1057/jibs.2014.68.

Stahl, G., Angwin, D. N., Very, P., Gomes, E., Weber, Y., Tarba, S. Y., et al. (2013). Sociocultural integration in mergers and acquisitions: Unresolved paradoxes and directions for future research. *Thunderbird International Business Review, 55*(4), 333–356. https://doi.org/10.1002/tie.

Stahl, G. K., Tung, R. L., Kostova, T., & Zellmer-Bruhn, M. (2016). Widening the lens: Rethinking distance, diversity, and foreignness in international business research through positive organizational scholarship. *Journal of International Business Studies, 47*(6), 621–630. https://doi.org/10.1057/jibs.2016.28.

Teerikangas, S. (2012). Dynamics of acquired firm pre-acquisition employee reactions. *Journal of Management, 38*(2), 599–639. https://doi.org/10.1177/0149206310383908.

Teerikangas, S., & Irrmann, O. (2016). Cultural change following international acquisitions: Cohabiting the tension between espoused and practiced cultures. *Management International Review, 56*(2), 195–226. https://doi.org/10.1007/s11575-015-0276-1.

Teerikangas, S., & Very, P. (2006). The culture–performance relationship in M&A: From yes/no to how. *British Journal of Management, 17*(SUPPL. 1). https://doi.org/10.1111/j.1467-8551.2006.00477.x.

Tran, V. (1998). The role of the emotional climate in learning organisations. *The Learning Organization, 5*(2), 99–103.

Weber, Y., & Drori, I. (2011). Integrating organizational and human behavior perspectives on mergers and acquisitions. *International Studies of Management and Organization, 41*(3), 76–95. https://doi.org/10.2753/IMO0020-8825410305.

Whetten, D., & Cameron, K. (2011). *Developing management skills* (8th ed.). Boston: Prentice Hall.

Xie, E., Reddy, K. S., & Liang, J. (2017). Country-specific determinants of cross-border mergers and acquisitions: A comprehensive review and future research directions. *Journal of World Business, 52*(2), 127–183. https://doi.org/10.1016/j.jwb.2016.12.005.

CHAPTER 4

Finding Continuity in a Serial Acquirer

Abstract This chapter focuses on the acquiring company. The data was collected from a 30-year-old company, which, during its life course, has undergone both a change from family ownership to investor ownership and rapid growth through a series of acquisitions. During this turmoil, the organizational identity and strategy have changed, causing organizational and emotional disorder. Thus, this chapter explores the connection between employee emotions and concerns over organizational identity, asking how acquiring organizations can signal continuity following acquisitions. Post-acquisition change is recognized as a potential identity threat, often leading employees to adopt protectionist attitudes. Nevertheless, based on social identity theory and organizational socialization, it is possible for companies to encourage organizational identification. Building on these notions, this chapter suggests how organizations can increase perceptions of continuity when undergoing constant change.

Keywords Organizational identity • Serial acquirer • Continuity

R. Harikkala-Laihinen, *Managing Emotions in Organizations*,
https://doi.org/10.1007/978-3-030-60567-4_4

1 Introduction

Organizational identity refers to the features of the organization that can be considered central, distinctive and enduring (Albert and Whetten 1985; Ashforth and Mael 1996)—the collective understanding of who *we* are (Raitis 2015). Such anthropomorphism, reflecting who we are rather than what the company is, enables the organization to develop a kind of personality, which facilitates a more memorable, engaging and motivating identity (Ashforth et al. 2020). In effect, attributing human features to an organization allows it to become more familiar, tangible and understandable, something real, which can be known and thus identified with (Ashforth and Mael 1996). This power stems from the fact that organizations are inherently human entities and thus reflect human processes of thought and behaviour (Ashkanasy et al. 2017). The attempt to build a shared identity among the involved employees is also a crucial part of post-acquisition integration (Dao and Bauer 2020).

However, when an acquisition prompts major organizational restructuring, organizational identity may become threatened (e.g. Menges and Kilduff 2015; Raitis et al. 2017). More particularly, when integration is seen as changing the identity of the pre-acquisition organization or its sub-groups, employees tend to react with insecurity and resistance (Dao and Bauer 2020). In general, such threat perceptions arise when employees perceive the acquisition as potentially making things worse for them. This can occur, for example, through potential downsizing threatening unemployment or the loss of colleagues, or a reallocation of resources threatening development opportunities or prompting relocation (Biggane et al. 2017). Change seems to attack how the accustomed identity is to endure, raising worries over the continuity of what is central and distinctive about it. These worries are likely heightened when an organization undergoes a series of potentially threatening events, as is the case for serial acquirers—organizations that acquire several companies over a limited period. Thus, this chapter addresses the question, *how can acquiring organizations signal continuity following acquisitions?*

For organizational identification to persist following an acquisition, a perception of continuity is essential. Nevertheless, employees often feel the change is so vast that the post-acquisition organization cannot be called the same company anymore. While employees accept that change is inevitable and can be beneficial for the organization, they miss the assurance and feeling that even after change, the company they work for will essentially be the same—it will be their organization. In effect, an acquisition triggers a sense of discontinuity, where employee comfort calls for continuity. Thus, an acquisition can prompt feelings of de-identification (van Knippenberg et al. 2002).

Because emotions can reveal what the members of an organization consider important (cf. Humphrey et al. 2015), this chapter argues that emotional identification is a key element in achieving the objective of continuity (cf. Raitis et al. 2017). In exploring the existing literature, this chapter therefore focuses on features that offer employees the chance to perceive change as affirmative and engage in change-congruent behaviour. In doing so, this chapter aims to bridge the long-lasting focus on detecting and dissolving identity threats with active attempts to encourage identification. This approach answers the call for considering the interconnections between group emotions and social identity (Ashkanasy et al. 2017).

2 Identity Following Acquisitions

2.1 Identity and Identification

Identity refers to the meanings given to the self. Thus, it structures and feeds the self-concept, anchoring the self to wider social spheres (Gecas 1982). Consequently, work-related identity refers to the construction of the self in the work domain (Dutton et al. 2010). Organizational identity, who *we* are, reflects employees' shared perceptions of what the organization is (Ashforth and Mael 1996). This chapter focuses on the collective organizational identity. The central attributes of an organization become visible, for example, through values, practices and offerings. In identifying the central attributes, an organization's history is important, as it enables the evaluation of the congruency of the organization's actions to its identity. What makes the organizational identity distinctive is what members perceive as separating it from other organizations. What makes the identity enduring is continuation over time—or a perception thereof (Gioia et al. 2013).

Social identity theory posits that social actors wish to see themselves as one with a social group; being similar to other members of the group and perceiving events from the perspective of the group (Stets and Burke 2000). Whereas identity theory focuses on the micro-sociological individual level, social identity theory draws on social psychology to explain collective processes and intergroup relationships (Hogg et al. 1995).

Correspondingly, social identity refers to the part of an individual's self-concept, which is directly linked to the group membership that the individual values cognitively and emotionally (Tajfel 1982), although social identity theory largely highlights the emotional element in identity and identification (Johnson et al. 2012). Social identity connotes a collective self-concept. Thus, organizational identity refers to members' perceptions about the core attributes of the company, as opposed to a construed external image of what outsiders think of the company (Piening et al. 2020; cf. Dutton et al. 1994). The perception of the self as part of a social group acts as a basis for the attitudes and behaviours that become predominant in the group (van Knippenberg et al. 2002).

Language, the creation of words, which give meaning to collective experiences, can help identity creation and act as an anchor for employees' emotions and perceptions (Pettigrew 1979). A sense of who *we* are at the base of organizational identity helps employees think, feel and act in ways that correlate with the identity, because is accentuates a sense of a collective self. Whereas many organizational characteristics that are central, distinctive and enduring could be described in terms of *what* (e.g. established, bureaucratic), considering the attributes of *who* gives them much more life and meaning (e.g. old, slow). Because of the strength in such an anthropomorphism, organizations may want to utilize one of three available strategies to promote this sense of *who* in the organization. First, they can say it by explicitly promoting what is human-like in the organization and speaking with the voice of the organization. Second, they can show it by acting in ways that promote the human-like attributes of the organization, in effect, walking the talk. Third, they can stage it by setting up opportunities for members to engage with the human-like attributes of the organization (Ashforth et al. 2020).

Organizational identification refers to the perception of belonging to or being one with an organization (Mael and Ashforth 1992), and thereby defining oneself in terms of the organization. In effect, based on social identity theory, organizational identification refers to a shared identity within an organization (Ashforth and Mael 1989). The stronger the identification, the greater the tendency to adopt the attributes that define the organization to define the self. Thus, organizational identification reflects a psychological attachment to the organization (Dutton et al. 1994). Seeing as human behaviour, and thereby organizational behaviour, stems from two sources, cognition and affect (Ashkanasy et al. 2017), organizational identification can also be seen as stemming from either a cognitive or an emotional origin. The difference lies between the difference in perceiving (cognitive) and feeling (affective, emotional) oneness (Johnson et al. 2012). In this chapter, the focus is on the affective emotional level.

In settings where one group is focal and others are adjoining, adjoining group members will anchor their perceptions to the focal parts if the focal group is considered to be within meaningful group boundaries. However, in these situations, strengthening group identity can make the boundaries between groups more rigid (Kahn et al. 2018). This is visible, for example, in the dual organizational identification with the core company and its local subsidiary seen in multinational corporations (Smale et al. 2015). Following an acquisition, the separate organizational groups may experience in-group bias, thwarting them from adapting to a new identity (van Leeuwen et al. 2003; cf. Menges and Kilduff 2015). Nevertheless, an integration strategy may make identification with the pre-acquisition organization possible for employees of the dominant party (van Knippenberg et al. 2002). Overall, when the post-acquisition identity is seen as a continuation of the pre-acquisition identity, identification becomes easier. At the same time, continuity of the pre-acquisition identity may increase in-group bias, effecting perceived deviance in the out-group, often reflecting the acquisition partner (van Leeuwen et al. 2003).

2.2 *Emotions and Identity*

Emotional identification with an organization refers to the members' emotional attachment to the organization and the emotions that arise as a consequence of the organization and membership therein (Raitis et al. 2017). Identity and identification is enduring because members create an emotional bond to the collective and to the mutual benefits it offers. Identification creates feelings of attachment, which turn into positive behaviour such as loyalty (Huy 1999). Due to the need to establish belongingness and the resulting tendency to form social attachments (Baumeister and Leary 1995), emotional attachment also correlates with the strength of organizational identification (Pratt 2000). In contrast, a lack of such emotional attachment is detrimental to well-being (Baumeister and Leary 1995).

As a majority of the identity literature to date has focused on threats to identity (Raitis et al. 2017), many negative emotions have been found to have a relationship with identity. For example, jealousy prompted by perceived favouritism can thwart employees' sense of identity (Andiappan and

Dufour 2020). Similarly, *schadenfreude* (epicaricacy) can strengthen identification with the in-group (Li et al. 2019), lowering the willingness to identify with a new entity. In contrast, systemic shame is a source of disciplinary power, directing behaviour towards praiseworthy behaviour in order to maintain group membership (Creed et al. 2014). Moreover, a sense of loss and grief can thwart identity transition altogether (Conroy and O'Leary-Kelly 2014).

A more recent research stream focuses on positive identity, highlighting understanding positive identity construction beyond the responses to identity threats (Dutton et al. 2010). For example, a shared identity can encourage positive behaviour such as trust formation and cooperation. In addition, identification increases affective attachment to the group (Williams 2001). Identification also increases commitment and engages employees in organizational citizenship behaviour (Cardon et al. 2017). A positive organizational identity encourages employees to behave in ways that stimulate positive organizational outcomes. Constructing a positive identity can also drive institutional change (Dutton et al. 2010).

A change in identity can trigger strong emotional reactions, which influence the way we behave during and perceive the change (Huy 1999). Change receptiveness refers to attitudes set between passive acceptance and active endorsement, whereas change resistance varies between inactive withdrawal and active resistance (Huy 1999; Oreg et al. 2018). Negative emotions are likely to lead to change resistance, whereas positive emotions enable change receptiveness (cf. Lazarus 1993; Oreg et al. 2018; Harikkala-Laihinen 2019). During change, employees' behavioural responses are often directly linked to their emotional responses. A change triggers a cognitive appraisal of its favourability for the self and for the work group one identifies with, leading to neutral, positive, negative, or mixed perceptions. This evaluation then leads to the corresponding behaviour, moderated by the perceived implications of potential behavioural patterns (Smollan 2006).

2.3 *Identity-Conscious Change*

An acquisition prompts the re-categorization of previously separate groups into a new joint group. As the new group maintains features and attributes of the former group, it can be seen as a continuation of the old group. However, it is essentially a new group, as it includes new members. Thus, a post-acquisition identity harbours features of both old and new, making the context particularly interesting (van Knippenberg et al. 2002).

Identity reflects the need of all social actors to harbour a sense of self, to portray a fundamental image of who *we* are (Gioia et al. 2013). Identifying as a collective *we* is socially comforting and enables employees to make sense of the company. Thus, employees are willing to identify with an organization that they consider relatable. This identification includes the recognition of cues regarding the attributes of the organization, the perception of the cues' centrality and the projection of the cues from the self (Ashforth et al. 2020). A change in identity occurs through identity transitions, where a period of liminality represents a dynamic shift from who I was to who am I becoming. The failure to make this transition results in becoming consumed by a sense of loss and an inability to let go of the old self (Conroy and O'Leary-Kelly 2014). In the worst-case scenario, letting go of the established identity attributes feels similar to death or nothingness (Huy 1999).

Liminality involves three phases: separation from the old identity, transition to the intermediate state of making sense of the attributes of the new identity and reincorporation to establish a new sense of identity (Conroy and O'Leary-Kelly 2014). Considering post-acquisition integration as a human change process includes the realization that all human change includes a psychological process of unlearning and relearning; the cognitive rebuilding and restructuring of ideas, perceptions and emotions. In order to be able to unlearn, in effect in order to be ready and motivated for change, disconfirmation of hopes or expectations is often the first step. For such disconfirmation to prompt change, it must trigger anxiety in terms of achieving future goals and thereby a wish to change in order to perform better. This is extremely difficult, as a willingness to change is related to a realization of imperfection, and even to a potential loss of self-esteem and identity. Therefore, the creation of psychological safety is essential. Balancing the disconfirmation with psychological safety allows individuals to accept the need to change. For example, group work, practice opportunities, establishing steps and objectives, coaching and creating a positive vision can help establish psychological safety around change (Schein 1996).

Employee participation has been identified as a key requisite for organizational transformation (Abildgaard et al. 2018; Harikkala-Laihinen 2019). In this respect, change can be defined as learning, and identity change following an acquisition may best be realized through managed learning (Schein 1996). Giving employees the chance to create shared meaning is essential in bringing about a new order and helping employees find their new role (Huy 1999). Because the objective of change is often pre-designed by company management, employees may mainly influence how the objective is reached. Nevertheless, as employees are often the best experts regarding daily work, including them in the process is essential. Their participation may be planned or prompted in the moment by the employees, and it can be direct or occur via representatives. However, what is more important is the purpose of the participation—whether employees are invited to participate to reach a set objective, or if the participation is an end in itself. While the former reflects a change process with a beginning and an end, the latter reflects the endorsement of participation in the workplace more broadly (Abildgaard et al. 2018).

One way to engage employees in the process is through socialization. Traditionally, socialization refers to newcomers entering an organization and learning their role within it (van Maanen and Schein 1979; Ashforth and Saks 1996). Arguably, these conditions are present when integration aims at creating a new whole from previously separate organizations (Harikkala-Laihinen 2019). Whereas formal institutionalized socialization teaches newcomers to maintain the status quo, more informal and personalized means can help individuals adopt their own role and approach to the job. Questioning a newcomer's identity may prompt a change in that identity, and particularly, collective socialization can encourage changes in beliefs and attitudes, increasing conformity with group norms. Thus, socialization drives identification (Ashforth and Saks 1996). Failure to socialize individuals may cause identity lingering; the continuity of an old identity, which is carried over from role to role. Moreover, continuous change may hinder an individual's ability to detect a role change or identity discontinuity. To encourage employees to accept the new identity, organizations should offer rites of passage and encourage employees to see change as definite (Wittman 2019).

Nevertheless, organizational evolvement can prompt employees' identity claim modification. While the central features of the identity may be maintained over time, it can adapt to new contexts and demands (Fisher et al. 2016). Beyond seeing organizational identity as enduring, it could therefore be claimed that organizational identity is dynamic (Gioia et al. 2013). For identity change to be successful, employees must be given the chance to reflect on the past and develop a new sense of the future. In effect, time for a mourning period over the old identity may be necessary.

This allows an emotional release of the old identity to happen and renews receptivity to the new identity. A new beginning can only be successful if the employees are able to see the change as justified (Huy 1999).

3 Method

3.1 A Brief History of Sigma

Sigma was established in Finland approximately 30 years ago[1] and operates in the high-tech industry. In the beginning, the company was owned by a sole entrepreneur and employed a team of approximately ten employees. After the first decade or so, essentially through a transfer to the next generation, the company became a growth-oriented family business. Both organic growth and growth through acquisitions occurred, but the acquired companies were not integrated. Instead, they were left essentially as stand-alone companies under Sigma's umbrella. During the next decade, Sigma grew from a small local player to a medium-sized multi-regional company, employing some 120 workers.

Sigma's newfound growth orientation meant that after some time, resources for growth became scarce. Thus, the company was sold to corporate investors a few years before its 30th birthday. After the change in ownership, transformation was fast. New companies were bought again and Sigma grew to employ some 300 workers. The corporate investor ownership also meant changes in the management of the company. The former family members soon left Sigma, and new management started to drive the unification of the company, essentially integrating all of the previously bought firms into Sigma along with newer purchases. While this turmoil was ongoing, research cooperation was established in autumn 2019 to explore Sigma's identity throughout the years.

3.2 Data Collection and Analysis

Data collection at Sigma occurred through semi-structured interviews focusing on features of the company that the employees saw as central, their experience of the working atmosphere at Sigma and the changes the employees considered significant in Sigma's life cycle. The purpose of the interviews was to reveal in-depth information regarding the company

[1] To protect Sigma's anonymity, the exact years of operation are not revealed.

context and employee perceptions (cf. Saldaña 2011). The semi-structured nature of the interviews ensured the comparability and value of the interviews (cf. Tolley et al. 2016). For example, the interviews posed general questions regarding the nature of Sigma as an employer, Sigma's meaning to the interviewee personally and the interviewee's perception of Sigma's purpose. The interview topics and questions were kept relatively loose to allow the interviewees freedom in their responses.

As significant change events during Sigma's life cycle were expected to have influenced employees' identity perceptions, the interviews utilised the critical incident technique (CIT). The CIT allows the systematic collection of observed significant incidents. Following the key steps of the CIT as described by Flanagan (1954), the interviewees were asked to identify significant events over the company's life cycle and place them on a company timeline. The interviewee was then asked to identify the most significant event, and describe how that event came to be, who was involved, how the event influenced Sigma and their job at Sigma, and other relevant information that might increase the understanding of the event. A similar approach has previously been successfully adopted by Durand (2016) to explore managerial emotions following acquisitions.

The interviewees, 24 altogether, were chosen to represent myriad functions, hierarchical levels, employment lengths and locations at Sigma (Table 4.1). To protect the anonymity of the company and the interviewees, the locations are not revealed. Nevertheless, recent acquisitions and those belonging to former umbrella companies that were recently integrated are highlighted. The interviews lasted approximately between 30–60 minutes and were audio-recorded to enable transcription. Most of the interviews were conducted face-to-face at the interviewees' offices, but due to long distances, two were conducted over Microsoft Teams. All of the interviews were conducted in Finnish, the mother tongue of both the interviewer and the interviewees.

The analysis of the interview findings was aided by QSR NVivo software. First, careful notes taken during the interviews were read thoroughly to gain an understanding of the whole. Based on this reading, very few theory-led categories were used, as more meaningful categories seemed to arise from the data. Nevertheless, theory-led headings of life cycle, identity, management, employer and emotions were used to categorize the emergent themes. The interview transcriptions produced several subcategories, of which the need for development, leadership, atmosphere, Sigma's character, communication, turmoil and the future were most

Table 4.1 Sigma interviews

Function	*Employment (years)*	*Acquisition or integration*	*Duration*
Development Manager	1–2	Integrated	42 min
Finance	>10	–	62 min
Finance	3–5	–	57 min
Human Resources	3–5	Integrated	67 min
Human Resources	1–2	2018	53 min
Human Resources	1–2	–	62 min
Marketing	6–10	2017	40 min
Marketing	>10	2018	65 min
Production Manager	3–5	2016	55 min
Production Manager	3–5	2017	42 min
Production Manager	1–2	Integrated	54 min
Production, expert services	>10	2018	51 min
Production, logistics	3–5	–	55 min
Production, logistics	1–2	–	55 min
Production, logistics	1–2	Integrated	43 min
Production, projects	<1	–	60 min
Production, support	1–2	Integrated	39 min
Production, support	<1	–	39 min
Sales	>10	–	58 min
Sales	>10	–	58 min
Sales	6–10	Integrated	29 min
Sales	6–10	2014	56 min
Sales	3–5	Integrated	54 min
Sales	1–2	–	54 min

significant. To highlight the significant events the interviewees identified, the timelines they produced were combined and an image of significant periods at Sigma, as defined by the identified events, was formulated.

4 Identity Turmoil at Sigma

4.1 Sigma's Life Cycle

Based on the interviewee-drawn timelines and corresponding discussions, Sigma's life cycle so far has had three significant phases: founding, family growth and a fresh start (Fig. 4.1). Whereas the founding era lasted approximately a decade, the family growth era was somewhat longer, ending in the ownership change some four years ago.

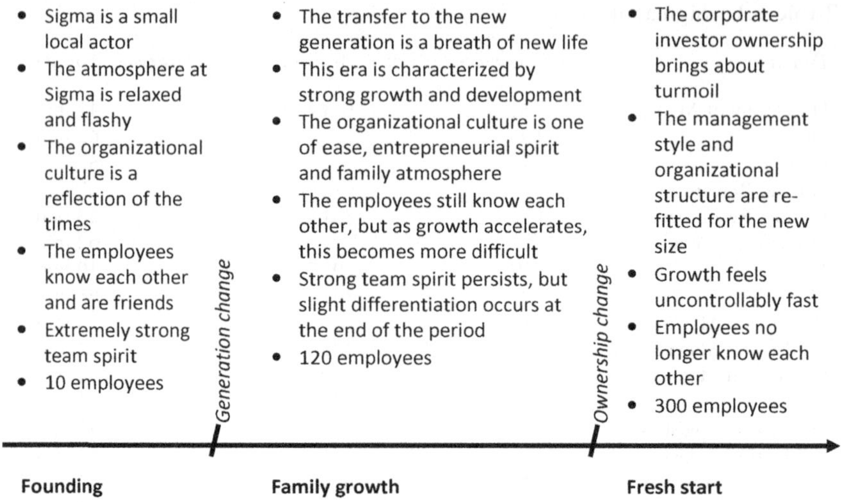

Fig. 4.1 Sigma's life cycle

The very beginning of Sigma was under the umbrella of another company. Nevertheless, Sigma had a stand-alone role. The founder, Robert,[2] was an energetic manager who had an authoritative manner. He also portrayed the time, the early 1990s, in the organizational culture through rough humour and the old-time use of verbal force. Eventually an outside sales director replaced Robert, but did not last very long at the company. The first significant change occurred when ownership transferred to the founder's daughter Mary, whose husband James became the next CEO. The new owners were perceived as grounded family-focused people, with earned authority.

> *When James came in, we clearly became our own company, we were Sigma. And we started to take the company in what I thought was the right direction, we started to develop. Before, the previous management did not have such a strong focus, but then the focus of what we are doing became much clearer.*
> *(Sales, >10 years at the company)*

[2] The names of every individual mentioned in the discussion have been changed to protect their anonymity.

During its very first years, Sigma's offering was directed at both corporate and private customers, serving both at the same premises. However, during the family growth era, the focus became corporate and public sector customers, and the consumer market was slowly ended. At the same time, marketing efforts were increased. The first acquisitions and the growth orientation of Sigma was personified by James. The interviewees described Sigma at the time as a quilt of companies, all under the same name, but all slightly different and in their own geographical location. At this time, the founding location was clearly the most central one.

Overall, James was seen as a caring, good insightful manager, who had the best interests of the company and its employees at heart. He was seen to lead by example and the interviewees perceived that during this era, the employees were taken into consideration, that they were heard. During the family growth era, Sigma felt like a small close-knit community. This established an emotional bond to the company as well as to colleagues. The entrepreneurial spirit of the owning family rubbed off on the employees, and reciprocity between the owners wanting to do their best for the employees and the employees wanting to do their best for the owners existed. The owners were always present, working alongside the employees, and the hierarchy was very low. The employees were trusted and had a sense of autonomy in their work. The next significant era at Sigma only started when the company was sold to a corporate investor.

> *In the beginning it was quite a shock, somehow frightening, because I immediately thought OK, now my job is gone.*
> *(Finance, 3–5 years at the company)*

The change in ownership was seen as the biggest single event by most interviewees due to the subsequent changes it prompted, for example, in management and the structure of the organization. It increased Sigma's resources and brightened the future in terms of investment opportunities. Nevertheless, particularly James leaving the company was a heavy blow to many who had been with Sigma for years. For some, Sigma had been the first and only employer of their lives, and the good atmosphere of the family growth era had correlated very strongly with James's presence at the company. The employees did understand that after investing everything—at least figuratively speaking—in Sigma for so long, James deserved a break and a new start of his own. Nevertheless, the change felt very personal.

This year we have suffered two great losses when both Mary and James have left us. This has been mentally really tough for me. They were both such great leaders, such wonderful people. Before I felt like I was working for them, it was more personal.—It feels somehow like … like in two years, their entire life's work has gone up in flames. And it feels awful, so awful.
(Finance, >10 years at the company)

Whereas the previous CEO James had a rather personal leadership style, the new CEO Michael was perceived as more of a generalist. Having no legacy at Sigma, he was possibly more perceptive of the bigger picture and did not have a location-based bias. Michael's different history put him in a better position to unite Sigma. The process of integrating all of the previously separate companies fully into Sigma was personified somewhat in Michael and in a few members of the new top-management team. The integration included a change in the organizational structure and a unification of systems and procedures. The purpose of the change was to create unity among the different locations, leading to the adoption of cross-location teams as the basis of different functions at Sigma. Besides creating internal unity, this renewal was seen as a way to increase the power of Sigma as a national-level player.

Our procedures have changed, and we have grown from garage nerds to a proper business that needs to be taken seriously, also in terms of our offering.
(Sales, 3–5 years at the company)

One significant change, along with integration, was to create a new look for Sigma. In effect, this meant a facelift to the logo, the creation of cartoon characters based on some of the employees to use in internal and external communications, and a switch to a unified office look in every location. In some locations, this meant a physical move to new offices, which was seen mostly as a positive development in terms of building unity. Nevertheless, for some, the switch to a flexi-office with no assigned desk was difficult, increasing distance working.

Everyone called the old offices the Funhouse. Upstairs, if you let a pencil go at one end, it would roll to the other end. There are still offices there, it hasn't been demolished or anything. It was just so funny, and we didn't have a fully open plan. Everyone had his or her own place, I liked that much better.
(Production, logistics, 3–5 years at the company)

While progress was perceived to be happening, the road ahead seemed long to most interviewees. Overall, many interviewees experienced a sense of turmoil, of rapid change at an uncontrollable pace. Some interviewees described the current situation as akin to working at a start-up. In addition, many perceived some change resistance, for example, vocal preferences for the old systems, thus making the fresh start era feel rather heavy. The employees also perceived that management was not listening to their concerns adequately and that the new organizational structure was leading the company into separate silos.

Nevertheless, this current era was underlined by the knowledge that a corporate investor would not remain the owner forever. Thus, a new change in ownership was looming somewhere on the horizon. While most interviewees saw the future of Sigma as positive, this change in ownership caused some worries. Many considered that the best-case scenario would be a new era of family growth, whereas the worst would be amalgamation with a big faceless group and a slow fading away. Particularly the personality of customer services was raised as a determinant of the brightness of the future, as a personalized service was seen as a way to distinguish Sigma from its competitors.

4.2 *Areas in Need of Attention*

Many described the leadership at Sigma as well meaning, but somewhat detached from the everyday work. The interviewed management-level personnel all mentioned their own willingness to learn and improve Sigma, but simultaneously saw many areas of development. Planning well enough and finishing one change before introducing another were mentioned as potential corrections. The justification for the changes was also lacking, particularly on the grass roots level. Dividing the changes into smaller, more digestible bits and making the process more concrete were suggested as corrections. Every interviewee also mentioned their appreciation of their immediate supervisor. Particularly the coaching style of management introduced in the fresh start era was mentioned as a good endeavour.

> *A good supervisor trusts you and doesn't try to micromanage. So that we can do our job in peace, with no one meddling, and we have the authority to make decisions about our job, that is very important in my opinion. That we ask, if there are any problems, and get help from the supervisor if we need it.*
> *(Production, logistics, 1–2 years at the company)*

HRM at Sigma was mainly praised, apart from some individual layoffs that were perceived as mishandled. Particularly the well-being efforts, including supporting recreational sports activities, were commended. Nevertheless, the function was relatively new, and was also being developed during the fresh start era, making it a novelty. While everyday work in HR seemed to function well, some uncertainty as to the purpose of the function remained.

> *My role in HR is somewhat difficult, because in a sense I can never really be part of the group. It is part of my job, that I cannot have a personal opinion. In HR, you can't play both sides, say one thing as a person and another with the voice of the company, that would become impossible.—In the beginning, this position raised some doubts because it was new.*
>
> *(Human Resources, 1–2 years at the company)*

Similarly, top management remained quite distant for many, particularly for the employees who had been at Sigma under the previous owners and who worked very closely with them. The hierarchy seemed much higher to some than others, and the decisions made about some of the process renewals were perceived as detached from what the job actually meant, making it impossible to follow the new rules.

> *Management has remained a bit alien to me; I don't really know them so well that I could analyse it. Before when I was working with James, who was our CEO, we worked closely together, it was very clear. Now maybe the addition of the middle people, the business area managers, we work with them much more than with top management.*
>
> *(Sales, >10 years at the company)*
>
> *Michael seems a bit passive. But then again, I don't know what Michael's job description is, what he is supposed to do in this company. I don't know what he is supposed to be involved in.*
>
> *(Production, logistics, 3–5 years at the company)*

Some interviewees also felt that the new team structure and product catalogue ate away from the previous strength of personalized customer service. This was a negative development, as personalized service and relationship-building were seen as a key way in which to lower the importance of product prices in the customer relationship. Flexibility and being able to offer exactly what the customer needs were seen as the cornerstone of the success in the family growth era.

> *The customers are saying we are bigger, we are less flexible, it feels like we no longer take care of them. These kinds of things. This is the last message you ever want to receive from customers.*
> *(Sales, 6–10 years at the company)*

Communication raised many opinions, both positive and negative. On the one hand, the interviewees felt that communication was on good grounds, and that effective virtual communication was enough for the most part. On the other hand, some called for more face-to-face meetings and clearer signals that the unification of Sigma meant that everyone was equally valuable. Particularly knowing one's colleagues across location borders was seen as a key towards good cooperation. Not knowing one's colleagues was seen as decreasing community spirit. Despite the integration endeavour, most interviewees still saw signs of the Sigma-quilt that predated the new ownership. Silos were also perceived as team boundaries became stronger. For many, it seemed that the geographical location or one's team was the first, and Sigma as a whole only the second point of identification. For some acquired employees, the former company still felt like a family. The unification was not progressing as planned and the renewal of processes was perceived as very confusing. Even though the unification was seen as a way to ensure the same quality across location borders, most interviewees reported the need for more clarity and organization in realizing the change. However, in terms of identity, this was not seen solely as a problem.

> *It is somehow healthy also, it creates a sense of togetherness, as long as it does not feed unhealthy competition. I am sure there are still sub-cultures, and I think it would be better if they are not fully extinguished. I have experienced a subsidiary where the only truth was the headquarters and that was very poisonous. There must be a bit of leeway.*
> *(Development Manager, 1–2 years at the company)*

The atmosphere at Sigma was generally perceived as very relaxed, positive and supportive, but many saw it as deteriorating. Disappointments in decisions, fears of job losses and negative thoughts emerged. Job satisfaction was seen as a core element of good work, highlighting the worries about the deteriorating atmosphere. Helpfulness and good humour were also mentioned as important parts of a good atmosphere. Division between different locations and different pre-acquisition groups was also perceived as a reality, and that it deteriorated the overall Sigma spirit, as the human needs of psychological safety, trust and acceptance were not always adequately met. Frustration seemed to be increasing.

Many expressed the view that the history of Sigma should also be better known to newer employees and particularly the new top-management team. This was seen as a way to understand Sigma better, and seemed important to both older and newer employees. However, part of the importance of the history was slightly divisive. Whereas the former central location employees were experiencing a strong sense of loss, the umbrella location employees experienced a sense of inferiority. In general, the interviewees were calling out to be heard, as decision-making was perceived as distant. Recognizing the employees who were going above and beyond their job description was also called for. Whereas some interviewees saw the values of Sigma in their work, others were describing actions as violating the values. Particularly courage as a value seemed to be forgotten in many interviewees' opinions, and mistakes were stigmatized. Overall, the employees seemed largely divided.

4.3 The Changing Attributes of Sigma

Beyond the pay check, the interviewees were highly motivated by interesting versatile work tasks and the good atmosphere. Many also saw change and development opportunities as motivating. Sigma and belonging to Sigma were extremely valuable to most interviewees, particularly those who had stayed with the company for many years. The meaning of Sigma was more than an employer; it was a community. At best, Sigma was experienced as another family. This strong emotional attachment meant that when Sigma changed significantly, negative emotions such as grief emerged. Indeed, many changes were perceived at Sigma.

> *We are, all the time, living a revolution. But then again, one might say that change is permanent, and it just has to be accepted. In some companies the change pace is faster. We should remember where this company started, we are moving into a more organized direction all the time, but the journey is long, and many changes must happen in between.*
> *(Production Manager, 1–2 years at the company)*

The atmosphere had always felt very open to the interviewees, but that openness started to decrease during the fresh start era. For example, the communication lags that often accompany large-scale growth were visible. In addition, whereas some also saw the value "by way of joy" adopted in practice, others felt it represented mere words, not action. The growth brought with it decreased contacts, which increased perceptions of distance. In addition, the willingness to take risks seemed to decrease. Nevertheless, many experienced the new organizational structure as bringing clarity to job descriptions and responsibilities. This, along with the renewal and unification of systems and procedures was seen as an inherent part of growth, enabling cooperation across locations and functions. Still, the strong team- and function-based organizational structure also brought about a juxtaposition. In part, the changes were so vast that many were experiencing them as turmoil.

> *It's because I'm living in between, having seen the old, which I thought was so wonderful, and now I am in the midst of chaos.—But now things are starting to work out bit by bit.*
> *(Finance, 3–5 years at the company)*

During their employment, many interviewees had also noticed changes in themselves. For example, employees noted an increase in precision and that they were consciously adopting an attitude of calmness. Those in managerial positions perceived improvements in their supervisory capacity, partly due to Sigma's investment in a coaching style of leadership in the fresh start era. Due to growth, their job tasks also changed, either becoming more focused or shifting to new positions within the company. Some employees perceived an increase in creative and analytical work following the changes, which was welcomed. Many also reported increases in social and communication skills due to learning at work. Learning the ways of Sigma seemed to unite many of these experiences.

> *I think that according to Sigma's culture, I probably am a lot more relaxed than before, and I don't stress so much about certain things I used to stress about. It has been good for me, as even though I've never been burnt out, I've maybe been close a few times, when things have been tough.—Here, I think it's because of the people that we have such a good group of people, that's what makes it enjoyable.*
> *(Production Manager, 1–2 years at the company)*

Since the founding era and particularly during the family growth era, interviewees experienced a sense of *entrepreneurial spirit* at the core of Sigma. To some extent, this was also perceived as enduring, although the fresh start did dilute it somewhat. The entrepreneurial spirit was seen in the eagerness to take up tasks, the sense of autonomy and ambition. Being reliable, supporting longevity and inventiveness also reflected this spirit, whereas the continuous change in the field heightened its importance. This attribute was also reflected in the interviewees' perceptions of the purpose of Sigma as being profitable and as enabling meaningful work.

Another key feature of Sigma was *expertise*. This reflected one of the core values of Sigma mentioned during the interviews to be "the most skilled mate in town". Being customer-centric and flexible were particularly important to many interviewees. Tackling work with a hands-on attitude and being easily approachable stemmed from this objective, as did the wish for continuous development and learning. The use of modern tools and systems supported this attribute. Many interviewees also saw this as part of the purpose of Sigma—to help customers be successful and to make work easier for the customers.

Quirkiness and a start-up spirit were also mentioned by several interviewees; that Sigma dared to be a bit different, that it had a bit more personality. Being easy-going, social and positive were at the core of what Sigma membership meant to the interviewees. Openness, youthfulness, energy and eagerness characterized Sigma, and were visible, for example, in the adoption of the cartoon characters and the facelift given to the brand. Then again, this did not materialize into being too posh, but at the same time, Sigma remained unpretentious and authentic. This also echoed the wish to encounter customers on a personal level. This attribute was reflected in the interviewees' perception of the purpose of Sigma as being a renewing force in the field.

Although these three attributes—entrepreneurial spirit, expertise and quirkiness—were seen as central, distinctive and enduring, many interviewees expressed worries over their discontinuity. Sigma in the fresh start era was seen as more cautious and even as faceless. The humour and positive atmosphere that the employees appreciated were felt to have somewhat decreased.

4.4 Discussion

4.4.1 Identity and Identification at Sigma

It was clear that Sigma's identity was connected to the interviewees' self-concept, as they considered Sigma through their own experience and perception (cf. Gecas 1982; Dutton et al. 2010). On a collective level, Sigma had triggered a sense of who *we* are (cf. Ashforth and Mael 1996; Raitis 2015). The employees considered entrepreneurial spirit, expertise and quirkiness as the central, distinctive and enduring features of Sigma, reflecting Sigma's organizational identity (cf. Albert and Whetten 1985). The organization's history (cf. Gioia et al. 2013) was particularly visible in the entrepreneurial spirit and quirkiness attributes, as well as in the interconnections seen between Sigma's values and identity. The enduring nature of these attributes, while somewhat questioned in the current fresh start era, seemed a matter of perception rather than of immutability (cf. Gioia et al. 2013).

Based on the value placed on Sigma membership and the many notions of its family atmosphere, the interviewees experienced Sigma according to the principles of social identity theory (cf. Hogg et al. 1995; Stets and Burke 2000), also highlighting their identification and belongingness to Sigma (cf. Ashforth and Mael 1989; Mael and Ashforth 1992). One clear example of defining the self in terms of the organization's attributes (cf. Dutton et al. 1994) is the quotation mentioning the changes in the self according to Sigma's culture. It was clear from the interviewees' choice of words, such as "I feel", that the identity of Sigma and the employees' identification did connote a strong emotional aspect in addition to the more cognitive evaluation (cf. Tajfel 1982; Johnson et al. 2012). Similarly, the choice of words such as "we are" reflects the collective yet self-directed nature of a social identity (cf. Piening et al. 2020), and highlights how the perception of the self as belonging to a group triggers certain attitudes and behaviours (van Knippenberg et al. 2002).

The use of language, particularly in the formation of value statements such as "by way of joy" and "the most skilled mate in town" helped the employees to anchor their identity perceptions (cf. Pettigrew 1979) and promoted the human-like attributes of Sigma (Ashforth et al. 2020). Still, at the same time, it highlighted potential contradictions, as in the case of courage versus cautiousness. Nevertheless, the strong sense of *who we are* did help employees think, feel and act in ways that were congruent with Sigma's identity. Sigma was connected with attributes such as relaxed, energetic, quirky, skilled and so forth, making the identity perception much more tangible and meaningful. In many ways, walking the talk was also visible, as the employees did recognize these attributes in everyday work. Similarly, particularly some marketing efforts such as relaxed quirky customer events helped employees engage with the attributes (cf. Ashforth et al. 2020).

The division between the spheres of identification, either a location, a team, or Sigma as a whole, signals that what employees saw as the focal part gained much of their attachment (cf. Smale et al. 2015; Kahn et al. 2018). While some saw this as a potential problem, others experienced a mixture of identities as enrichening. The decisive factor seemed to be whether the in-group identification caused a strong bias against out-groups and prevented identification with the whole (cf. van Leeuwen et al. 2003; Menges and Kilduff 2015). The wish for continuity between pre- and post-acquisition organizational identity was clear at Sigma (cf. van Knippenberg et al. 2002; van Leeuwen et al. 2003). Thus, when changes in Sigma challenged the central, distinctive and enduring attributes, emotional confusion emerged.

4.4.2 Emotions Reflecting Sigma's Identity

The employees' emotional attachment to Sigma was clear. Many described Sigma as another family and detailed their emotions reflecting Sigma membership (cf. Raitis et al. 2017). The employees had clearly built a strong emotional bond with Sigma, which, on the one hand, helped Sigma's identity become enduring, triggering positive perceptions and loyalty (cf. Huy 1999), but, on the other hand, caused many negative perceptions when Sigma's identity was threatened. Indeed, it was clear that the stronger the emotional bond the employees seemed to harbour for Sigma, the stronger their identification with Sigma (cf. Pratt 2000). The very few employees who did not signal an emotional attachment to Sigma did seem to portray poorer work-related well-being (cf. Baumeister and Leary 1995), while at the same time, those who seemed to portray the strongest emotional attachment to Sigma seemed to also suffer the most when Sigma was perceived as changing.

During the turmoil of the fresh start era, Sigma employees experienced jealousy over perceived favouritism (cf. Andiappan and Dufour 2020), and portrayed a sense of loss and of grief that were clearly hindering their identity transition (cf. Conroy and O'Leary-Kelly 2014). Nevertheless, Sigma's identity was also seen as encouraging trust and cooperation, and clearly it encouraged attachment (cf. Williams 2001). Employees' identification with Sigma increased their commitment to the company and helped them act according to the norms of the company (cf. Cardon et al. 2017). Overall, while Sigma's identity mainly seemed to be positive (cf. Dutton et al. 2010), there were clear signals of a lowering of well-being, raising questions about the compatibility of the changes with Sigma's identity. Whereas many interviewees were in positive spirits, highly negative emotions also emerged (Fig. 4.2).

The employees' reactions were also clearly connected to how they perceived the change and behaved during the change (cf. Huy 1999; Smollan 2006; Oreg et al. 2018). A majority of the interviewees had a weak positive perception of the changes, accepting them but not really working towards them. Although they portrayed change receptiveness, they were not highly engaged in efforts to realize the change. The employees who saw change as highly positive and exciting were more willing to also act in ways that promoted change. The employees who saw change as slightly negative withdrew from efforts, whereas those who saw change as highly negative resisted it actively. However, it is important to note that active change resistance here refers to a more affective than behavioural process. The employees who experienced change at Sigma as highly negative mentally resisted the perceived change in Sigma's identity, but did not engage

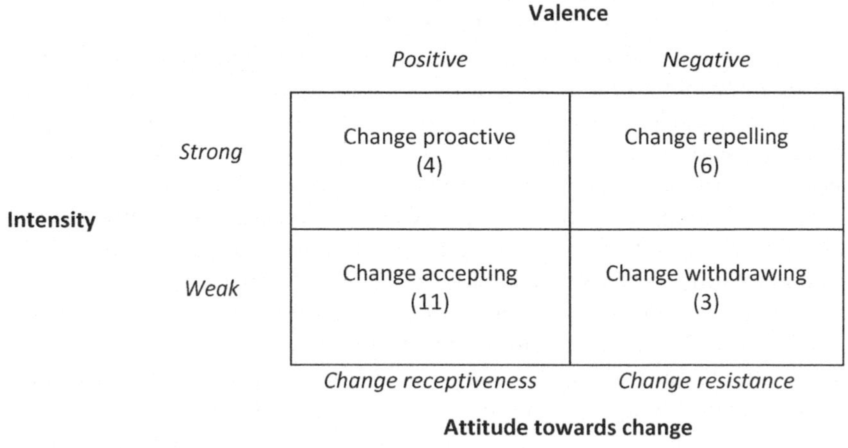

Fig. 4.2 Emotions at Sigma

in any behaviour undermining the change efforts. Consequently, it also seemed possible to promote change to those who saw it as an identity threat.

4.4.3 *Building a New Identity at Sigma*

Based on the employee experiences, Sigma's source of problems was in not recognizing the perceived majority of the change. Even though many years had passed since some of the employees were acquired, and others had never been acquired, essentially the unification of the fresh start era started an integration period, triggering highly emotional experiences (cf. Harikkala-Laihinen 2019). Although for many the unification of Sigma occurred not as a pure post-acquisition integration but as an organizational change process even years later, every employee experienced the change as essentially creating a new group, with features adopted from the old (cf. van Knippenberg et al. 2002). The necessity of building an image of *who we are* (e.g. Gioia et al. 2013) was clearly felt by the employees, who reported feelings of confusion when Sigma's identity was changing. This also highlighted the role of an organizational identity as a source of social comfort and sensemaking (cf. Ashforth et al. 2020). Based on the employees' feelings of confusion and turmoil, an identity transition—a sense of who Sigma members were becoming—was evident. It was equally perceptible that for some, the sense of loss was overwhelming (cf. Conroy and O'Leary-Kelly 2014), signalling that a badly managed identity transition period generates feelings of emptiness (cf. Huy 1999).

Sigma seemed firmly in the stage of liminality: the period of transition between an old and a new identity. Separation from the old identity had begun with the perceived changes, and the intermediate state of trying to make sense of what the new identity entailed was ongoing. What employees seemed to struggle with was the reincorporation of Sigma's attributes into a new identity (cf. Conroy and O'Leary-Kelly 2014). It was evident that the change at Sigma triggered a psychological process of unlearning and relearning, with a crucial emotional element of recreating the bond to a changed organization. Whereas disconfirmation had occurred through the perceived changes at Sigma, the future goals seemed too distant to motivate change. Thus, the danger of being stuck in a state of anxiety seemed plausible for many employees. As long as the old identity seemed more compelling, and could not be reconciled with the new, the willingness to change remained low. The only way to get around this dilemma seemed to be the creation of psychological safety in the new Sigma. Whereas a coaching management style was adopted to this end and the team structure offered chances of group work, no intermediate steps or objectives were introduced, and the employees did not have the opportunity to practice what the new Sigma meant. A positive vision did not emerge, meaning that psychological safety was not established as strongly as it could have been (cf. Schein 1996).

Organizational transformation could have been supported through designed efforts at creating shared meaning in the new Sigma (cf. Huy 1999; Harikkala-Laihinen 2019). At Sigma, the change was clearly directed by top management, meaning that employees only had the opportunity to influence the journey. However, what Sigma employees missed was the link between the change objectives and their application in everyday work. In effect, the employees were not clearly invited to participate in planning the changes, which triggered perceptions that the changes were incongruent with some work tasks. At Sigma, the change processes seemed to necessitate inviting employees to participate to reach the set objectives (cf. Abildgaard et al. 2018).

Essentially, the missing link seemed to centre on socialization (cf. van Maanen and Schein 1979; Ashforth and Saks 1996; Harikkala-Laihinen 2019). Both formal and informal socialization efforts might have eased the change, as formal efforts would have made the new features of Sigma more familiar to the employees, whereas the informal efforts would have helped create a new community spirit. Particularly collective socialization may have eased the transformation of employees' beliefs and attitudes, and thus encouraged identification with the new Sigma (cf. Ashforth and Saks 1996). Identity lingering seemed evident; many employees spoke of the good old times. Similarly, the constant turmoil meant that some employees did not have time to perceive what their role in the new Sigma meant. Thus, rites of passage, such as new orientation workshops for all employees, could have helped to encourage change acceptance and complete the identity transition (cf. Wittman 2019).

Another key opportunity Sigma seemed to miss was to encourage identity claim modification instead of a full identity transition. The new top management could have familiarized themselves with the history of Sigma in all the locations and across functions in order to recognize what corresponded in the central, distinctive and enduring features in all of them. Based on these discoveries, the old identity could have been maintained at the core of the new, even though it would have been adapted to a novel context with different demands (cf. Fisher et al. 2016). Indeed, the similarity between what the interviewees considered important and positive about Sigma reflects a high level of synchrony, indicating that unity could have been found and communicated. This reflects the dynamic nature of the enduring attributes over time (cf. Gioia et al. 2013).

Whereas Sigma management had the best of intentions in driving change, the necessity of letting the employees reflect on the past and offer them the basis to build an image of the future was not handled as well as it could have been. Apart from the means suggested above, because the employees did not have the chance to mourn for what was lost in the unification, the new identity never became as compelling as it could have become. In effect, many employees could not experience an emotional release that would have increased their receptivity to a new identity. Furthermore, the employees explicitly mentioned the low level of justification regarding the changes, indicating that without extra effort, a new beginning was likely to fail (Huy 1999).

5 Conclusion

This chapter has explored how acquiring organizations can signal continuity following acquisitions. The process of doing so was discovered to be inherently human, including both cognitive and emotional features (cf. Ashkanasy et al. 2017), but it is crucial in terms of building a shared identity (cf. Dao and Bauer 2020). When integration triggers perceptions of identity threats (cf. Menges and Kilduff 2015; Biggane et al. 2017; Raitis et al. 2017), insecurity and resistance emerge (cf. Dao and Bauer 2020). This highlights the need to emphasize the central, distinctive and enduring attributes of the organization (e.g. Ashforth and Mael 1996); in effect, the continuity of identity (cf. van Knippenberg et al. 2002).

Based on the literature review and the illustrative case example, there are several things organizations can do to ensure identity continuity following major restructuring. First, it is essential to recognize that a change in identity has been triggered. Even if the change seems minor, it may be perceived as major. Similarly, even if the change itself is positive, it may cause identity struggles, which are negative. Second, when identity change occurs, it is crucial that the change is seen all the way through so that the employees do not remain in a stage of liminality. Third, active efforts aimed at building shared meaning help employees identify with the new organization. Particularly socialization efforts are important in easing identity transition. Fourth, building the new identity based on already shared perceptions of what is central, distinctive and enduring helps highlight the continuity of the identity even when faced with adaptation to a new context. Finally, allowing the employees to mourn for perceived losses regarding their identity is essential in creating receptiveness to the new identity.

This chapter has shown how identification can be encouraged through active efforts even when identity threats occur. In identifying the means discussed above, this chapter has also shed light on how collective emotions are reflected in social identity. At Sigma, employee emotions clearly revealed the most important and valued parts of the organization (cf. Humphrey et al. 2015), indicating the importance of an emotional attachment to the organization (cf. Raitis et al. 2017). Moreover, this chapter has shown how identity change triggers slightly different change attitudes than the previous literature details. Whereas the previous organizational change literature (e.g. Waddell and Sohal 1998; Dhingra and Punia 2016; Oreg et al. 2018) highlights active change resistance and the anxiety, stress and anger it creates, highly negative attitudes regarding identity change do not necessarily activate employees against change per se. Instead, they cause the employees to repel the features of the new identity that seem to threaten the old identity and thereby the employees' self-conception. This means that the employees who struggle with identity-related change should not be perceived as actively change resistant, but as requiring the opportunity to mourn for the loss of their old identity in order to enable them to transition to the new.

References

Abildgaard, J. S., Hasson, H., von Thiele Schwarz, U., Løvseth, L. T., Ala-Laurinaho, A., & Nielsen, K. (2018). Forms of participation: The development and application of a conceptual model of participation in work environment interventions. *Economic and Industrial Democracy*, 1–24. https://doi.org/10.1177/0143831X17743576.

Albert, S., & Whetten, D. A. (1985). Organizational identity. *Research in Organizational Behavior, 7*, 263–295.

Andiappan, M., & Dufour, L. (2020). Jealousy at work: A tripartite model. *Academy of Management Review, 45*(1), 205–229. https://doi.org/10.5465/amr.2016.0299.

Ashforth, B. E., & Mael, F. (1989). Social identity theory and the organization. *The Academy of Management Review, 14*(1), 20–39. https://doi.org/10.2307/258189.

Ashforth, B. E., & Mael, F. (1996). Organizational identity and strategy as a context for the individual. *Advances in Strategic Management, 13*(1), 19–64.
Ashforth, B. E., & Saks, A. M. (1996). Socialization tactics: Longitudinal effects on newcomer adjustment. *The Academy of Management Journal, 39*(1), 149–178.
Ashforth, B. E., Schinoff, B. S., & Brickson, S. L. (2020). "My company is friendly," "mine's a rebel": Anthropomorphism and shifting organizational identity from "what" to "who". *Academy of Management Review, 45*(1), 29–57. https://doi.org/10.5465/amr.2016.0496.
Ashkanasy, N. M., Humphrey, R. H., & Huy, Q. N. (2017). Integrating emotions and affect in theories of management. *Academy of Management Review, 42*(2), 175–189.
Baumeister, R. F., & Leary, M. R. (1995). The need to belong: Desire for interpersonal attachments as a fundamental human motivation. *Psychological Bulletin, 117*(3), 497–529. https://doi.org/10.4324/9781351153683-3.
Biggane, J. E., Allen, D. G., Amis, J., Fugate, M., & Steinbauer, R. (2017). Cognitive appraisal as a mechanism linking negative organizational shocks and intentions to leave. *Journal of Change Management, 17*(3), 203–227. https://doi.org/10.1080/14697017.2016.1219379.
Cardon, M. S., Post, C., & Forster, W. R. (2017). Team entrepreneurial passion: Its emergence and influence in new venture teams. *Academy of Management Review, 42*(2), 283–305. https://doi.org/10.5465/amr.2014.0356.
Conroy, S. A., & O'Leary-Kelly, A. M. (2014). Letting go and moving on: Work-related identity loss and recovery. *Academy of Management Review, 39*(1), 67–87. https://doi.org/10.5465/amr.2011.0396.
Creed, W. E. D., Hudson, B. A., Okhuysen, G. A., & Smith-Crowe, K. (2014). Swimming in a sea of shame: Incorporating emotion into explanations of institutional reproduction and change. *Academy of Management Review, 39*(3), 275–301. https://doi.org/10.5465/amr.2012.0074.
Dao, M. A., & Bauer, F. (2020). Human integration following M&A: Synthesizing different M&A research streams. *Human Resource Management Review*, 1–19. https://doi.org/10.1016/j.hrmr.2020.100746.
Dhingra, R., & Punia, B. K. (2016). Relational analysis of emotional intelligence and change management: A suggestive model for enriching change management skills. *Vision, 20*(4), 312–322. https://doi.org/10.1177/0972262916668726.
Durand, M. (2016). Employing critical incident technique as one way to display the hidden aspects of post-merger integration. *International Business Review, 25*(1), 87–102. https://doi.org/10.1016/j.ibusrev.2015.05.003.
Dutton, J. E., Dukerich, J. M., & Harquail, C. V. (1994). Organizational images and member identification. *Administrative Science Quarterly, 39*(2), 239–263. https://doi.org/10.3233/CBM-130327.

Dutton, J. E., Roberts, L. M., & Bednar, J. (2010). Pathways for positive identity construction at work: Four types of positive identity and the building of social resources. *Academy of Management Review, 35*(2), 265–293. https://doi.org/10.5465/AMR.2010.48463334.

Fisher, G., Kotha, S., & Lahiri, A. (2016). Changing with the times: An integrated view of identity, legitimacy, and new venture life cycles. *Academy of Management Review, 41*(3), 383–409. https://doi.org/10.5465/amr.2013.0496.

Flanagan, J. (1954). The critical incident technique. *Psychological Bulletin, 51*(4), 327–358.

Gecas, V. (1982). The self-concept. *Annual Review of Sociology, 8*, 1–33.

Gioia, D. A., Patvardhan, S. D., Hamilton, A. L., & Corley, K. G. (2013). Organizational identity formation and change. *Academy of Management Annals, 7*(1), 123–193. https://doi.org/10.1080/19416520.2013.762225.

Harikkala-Laihinen, R. (2019). *The power of positivity: How employee emotions and interaction can benefit cross-border acquisitions.* Turku: University of Turku.

Hogg, M. A., Terry, D. J., & White, K. M. (1995). A tale of two theories: A critical comparison of identity theory with social identity theory. *Social Psychology Quarterly, 58*(4), 255–269. https://doi.org/10.2307/2787127.

Humphrey, R. H., Ashforth, B. E., & Diefendorff, J. M. (2015). The bright side of emotional labor. *Journal of Organizational Behavior, 36*(6), 749–769. https://doi.org/10.1002/job.

Huy, Q. N. (1999). Emotional capability, emotional intelligence, and radical change. *Academy of Management Review, 24*(2), 325–345. https://doi.org/10.5465/AMR.1999.1893939.

Johnson, M. D., Morgeson, F. P., & Hekman, D. R. (2012). Cognitive and affective identification: Exploring the links between different forms of social identification and personality with work attitudes and behavior. *Journal of Organizational Behavior, 33*(8), 1146–1167. https://doi.org/10.1002/job.

Kahn, W. A., Barton, M. A., Fisher, C. M., Heaphy, E. D., Reid, E. M., & Rouse, E. D. (2018). The geography of strain: Organizational resilience as a function of intergroup relations. *Academy of Management Review, 43*(3), 509–529. https://doi.org/10.5465/amr.2016.0004.

Lazarus, R. (1993). From psychological stress to the emotions: A history of changing outlooks. *Annual Review of Psychology, 44*, 1–21. https://doi.org/10.1146/annurev.psych.44.1.1.

Li, X., McAllister, D. J., Ilies, R., & Gloor, J. L. (2019). Schadenfreude: A counternormative observer response to workplace mistreatment. *Academy of Management Review, 44*(2), 360–376. https://doi.org/10.5465/amr.2016.0134.

Mael, F., & Ashforth, B. E. (1992). Alumni and their alma mater: A partial test of the reformulated model of organizational identification. *Journal of Organizational Behavior, 13*(2), 103–123. https://doi.org/10.1002/job.4030130202.

Menges, J. I., & Kilduff, M. (2015). Group emotions: Cutting the gordian knots concerning terms, levels of analysis, and processes. *Academy of Management Annals, 9*(1), 845–928. https://doi.org/10.1080/19416520.2015.1033148.

Oreg, S., Bartunek, J. M., Lee, G., & Do, B. (2018). An affect-based model of recipients' responses to organizational change events. *Academy of Management Review, 43*(1), 65–86. https://doi.org/10.5465/amr.2014.0335.

Pettigrew, A. M. (1979). On studying organizational cultures. *Administrative Science Quarterly, 24*(4), 570–581.

Piening, E. P., Salge, T. O., Antons, D., & Kreiner, G. E. (2020). Standing together or falling apart? Understanding employees' responses to organizational identity threats. *Academy of Management Review, 45*(2), 325–351. https://doi.org/10.5465/amr.2016.0457.

Pratt, M. G. (2000). The good the bad and the ambivalent: Managing identification among Amway distributors. *Administrative Science Quarterly, 45*(3), 456–493.

Raitis, J. (2015). *Identity and multinational corporations: Building unity within diversity*. Turku: University of Turku.

Raitis, J., Harikkala-Laihinen, R., Hassett, M., & Nummela, N. (2017). Finding positivity during a major organizational change: In search of triggers of employees' positive perceptions and feelings. In W. Zerbe, C. Härtel, N. Ashkanasy, & L. Petitta (Eds.), *Emotions and identity: Research on emotion in organizations* (Vol. 13, pp. 3–16). https://doi.org/10.1108/S1746-979120170000013001.

Saldaña, J. (2011). *Fundamentals of qualitative research*. Oxford: Oxford University Press.

Schein, E. H. (1996). Kurt Lewin's change theory in the field and in the classroom: Notes toward a model of managed learning. *Systems Practice, 9*(1), 27–47. https://doi.org/10.1007/BF02173417.

Smale, A., Björkman, I., Ehrnrooth, M., John, S., Mäkelä, K., & Sumelius, J. (2015). Dual values-based organizational identification in MNC subsidiaries: A multilevel study. *Journal of International Business Studies, 46*(7), 761–783. https://doi.org/10.1057/jibs.2015.18.

Smollan, R. (2006). Minds, hearts and deeds: Cognitive, affective and behavioural responses to change. *Journal of Change Management, 6*(2), 143–158. https://doi.org/10.1080/14697010600725400.

Stets, J. E., & Burke, P. J. (2000). Identity theory and social identity theory. *Social Psychology Quarterly, 63*(3), 224–237. https://doi.org/10.2307/2695870.

Tajfel, H. (1982). Social psychology of intergroup relations. *Annual Review of Psychology, 33*, 1–39. https://doi.org/10.1007/978-94-015-9245-1_7.

Tolley, E., Ulin, P. R., Mack, N., Robinson, E. T., & Succop, S. M. (2016). *Qualitative methods in public health: A field guide for applied research* (2nd ed.). San Francisco, CA: Jossey-Bass.

van Knippenberg, D., van Knippenberg, B., Monden, L., & de Lima, F. (2002). Organizational identification after a merger: A social identity perspective. *British Journal of Social Psychology, 41*(2), 233–252. https://doi.org/10.1348/014466602760060228.

van Leeuwen, E., van Knippenberg, D., & Ellemers, N. (2003). Continuing and changing group identities: The effects of merging on social identification and ingroup bias. *Personality and Social Psychology Bulletin, 29*(6), 679–690. https://doi.org/10.1177/0146167203251210.

van Maanen, J., & Schein, E. (1979). Toward a theory of organizational socialization. In B. Straw (Ed.), *Research in organizational behavior* (Vol. 1, pp. 1–89). New York: JIP Press.

Waddell, D., & Sohal, A. S. (1998). Resistance: A constructive tool for change management. *Management Decision, 36*(8), 543–548. https://doi.org/10.1108/00251749810232628.

Williams, M. (2001). In whom we trust: Group membership as an affective context for trust development. *Academy of Management Review, 26*(3), 377–396. https://doi.org/10.5465/AMR.2001.4845794.

Wittman, S. (2019). Lingering identities. *Academy of Management Review, 44*(4), 724–745. https://doi.org/10.5465/amr.2015.0090.

CHAPTER 5

Conclusion

Abstract This chapter discusses how each of the three cases portrays positive change management following acquisitions, detailing the theoretical and managerial insights that were uncovered. This chapter provides scholars with a map of interrelated emotion concepts and their connection to acquisition research, detailing how concepts such as emotion or emotional identification can be used in high-quality empirical research. This collection of concepts also acts as a guideline in choosing theoretical lenses for different types of acquisition studies considering employee emotions. Furthermore, this chapter highlights the practical guidelines for successful emotion management following acquisitions, detailing crucial points of attention with regard to managers, employee emotions, the emotional climate and identity. Finally, this chapter discusses the key limitations of the book and indicates fruitful future research directions.

Keywords Positive change management • Positive post-acquisition integration • Emotion management

R. Harikkala-Laihinen, *Managing Emotions in Organizations*,
https://doi.org/10.1007/978-3-030-60567-4_5

1 Returning to the Scene

This book has attempted to highlight the place for humanity in the bottom line of a company, not as a numeral, but as individuals, whose efforts have an undeniable influence on corporate performance. This book has paid particular attention to the emotions that pervade organizations (cf. Ashkanasy 2003), emphasizing the positive, unifying and enduring facets of organizational change following acquisitions. At the core of this book has been the need to highlight the ways in which to create positive attitudes (cf. Birkinshaw et al. 2000) that enable change receptiveness following acquisitions.

In Chap. 1, this book chose a cognitive appraisal theory definition of emotions, separating the concept from other affective states such as moods. Emotions were defined as episodes, which include a trigger, an appraisal of the trigger and a subsequent appraisal-congruent reaction (Fredrickson 2001). In addition, emotions were found to have a positive or negative valence (e.g. Russell and Carroll 1999), as well as activation tendencies (e.g. Ashkanasy and Dorris 2017). Furthermore, it was highlighted that at work, emotions appear on many levels (e.g. Ashkanasy 2003), and can become collective (e.g. Kemper 2002; Menges and Kilduff 2015). Most importantly, affective events were identified as the cause of emotional experiences at work (e.g. Weiss and Cropanzano 1996), whereas change was identified as a key emotion-triggering event (e.g. Kiefer 2005; Oreg et al. 2018).

On these grounds, this book has sought to increase conceptual clarity and balance the previous negative bias in acquisition research in order to shed light on positivity, collective emotion management and the emergence of group emotions following acquisitions. This concluding chapter recaps the key findings from each case study illustrated in the book, highlighting the summary conclusions and contributions to both the literature and practice.

2 The Many Faces of Positive

2.1 Positive Change Management in Each Case Study

Returning to the positive post-acquisition change steps identified in Chap. 2, although Alpha Group, Delta and Sigma all showed positive change management endeavours, the foci of these endeavours differed greatly between the companies (Table 5.1).

Table 5.1 Positive change management in each case study

Step	*Alpha group*	*Delta*	*Sigma*
Detect and understand employee emotions in order to encourage positivity	• Research cooperation centring on emotions • Employee survey to discover emotions • Value workshops to encourage positivity *Focus on discovering emotions*	• Research cooperation centring on emotions • Employee survey for evaluating employee well-being • Company meetings to encourage positivity *Focus on evaluating well-being*	• Research cooperation centring on identity • Employee survey to explore well-being • Team meetings to encourage identification *Focus on unity*
Communicate the positive aspects of integration, creating a sense of excitement and readiness	• Benefits from continuity, growth and internationalization • Excitement and readiness through engaging value work *Focus on the benefits of growth*	• Benefits from continuity and investments • Excitement and readiness through the continuity *Focus on the benefits of continuity*	• Benefits from growth • Benefits from operational synergies • Excitement and readiness through increased power *Focus on the benefits of size*
Form a compelling vision of the future of the integrated company	• Joint values guiding work *Focus on joint values as guidelines*	• Continued existence *Focus on continued existence*	• Operational synergies *Focus on increased economies and growth*
Respond to employees' emotions in ways that encourage commitment to the integrated company	• Increased communication based on research findings • Variety of communication means *Focus on increased interaction*	• Increased communication based on research findings • Variety of communication means *Focus on increased communication*	• Promotion of unity *Focus on the joint company*
Strengthen the achieved integration through encouraging employees to identify with the new organization	• Promoting the new company name • Adopting the values in the long-term vision *Focus on the joint organization*	• Parent company presence *Focus on the parent company*	• Promotion of synergy benefits • Promotion of growth *Focus on the change*

Whereas Alpha Group put emphasis on discovering employee emotions in order to tackle any underlying issues, Delta's focus centred more on evaluating employee well-being, whereas Sigma emphasized resultant unity. While all these objectives are positive in nature, Alpha Group's approach is perhaps most likely to generate feelings of engagement and care, which increase employee motivation to work towards change. In their communication, Alpha Group focused on detailing the mutual benefits of joint forces. This helped employees see the benefits of integration. However, at Delta, the focus of communication was continuity. Again, while this was extremely positive for Delta employees, it did not engage them in integration, but instead highlighted the pre-acquisition *us*. Similarly, at Sigma, the focus on growth and increased strength, while positive, may have remained somewhat distant from the employees' everyday work. Thus, it did not increase positivity as much as more engaging communication efforts may have done.

Continuity was also reflected in how Delta communicated a future vision. Longevity and continued existence were, of course, experienced as very positive, but again the message did not portray unity between Delta and Gamma. At Alpha Group, the compelling vision was built anew to include both pre-acquisition organizations. The new values were to guide mutually beneficial behaviour. This message portrayed unity and thus encouraged integration. Again, at Sigma, the objective of achieving increased economies of scale is highly beneficial, but is rather detached from the employees' everyday experience and particularly from their identification with the company. Thus, while it increased employee understanding of the benefits of change, it did not create readiness for change.

Through their efforts in detecting and understanding employee emotions, both Alpha Group and Delta were able to react to employee experiences. Alpha Group focused on interaction by inviting employees to breathe life into the new company values, whereas Delta focused on increased communication in order to alleviate worries. At Sigma, the focus lay on the benefits of unity. All these objectives were positive and helpful, but again, Alpha Group was best able to increase employee engagement during the integration. In contrast, Delta managed to create positivity towards the pre-acquisition organization. Sigma, in turn, did try to respond to employee concerns through pushing the change, but failed to take the employee reactions into consideration while the change was ongoing, thus allowing very different experiences and sub-cultures to be maintained.

Finally, Alpha Group sought to reinforce integration through promoting the post-acquisition organization, whereas Delta's efforts were put into presenting the parent company and Sigma's centred on the change objectives. These efforts again all portray positive endeavours, but Alpha Group's tactic proved most effective in terms of unification. At Delta, bridging the *us* and *them* necessitated more attention, while at Sigma, showing the links between the old and the new would have resulted in increased change receptiveness.

2.2 Building Positivity Following Acquisitions

Adhering to POS, this book has attempted to highlight how particularly positive contexts or actions can generate organizational success (e.g. Cameron et al. 2003; Cameron 2012). In doing so, this book has emphasized how reversing negative experiences is not enough to create positivity (cf. Roberts 2006). Thus, the focus of this book has been on the particular practices that can be adopted to increase positivity following acquisitions, as illustrated through the three case studies.

In building positive affirmative change (Avey et al. 2008), emphasizing positive emotion triggers (Cameron 2008) is essential. In effect, this occurs through highlighting events and attributes that generate positive emotions. Because group membership can trigger collective emotions (e.g. Goldenberg et al. 2014), perceived threats to the group often create protectionist attitudes (Menges and Kilduff 2015). Thus, managing collective emotions following acquisitions is crucial. Successful socialization through training sessions, social gatherings and formal information exchange (Larsson and Lubatkin 2001) offers one avenue for emotion management. Because employees tend to have very strong reactions to change (e.g. Cartwright and Cooper 1993), highlighting the positive outcomes related to the change is essential (cf. Teerikangas 2012).

Positive emotions also feed a positive emotional climate (Bar-tal et al. 2007), which enhances organizational identification and promotes cooperation (Fischer and Manstead 2008). What makes an emotional climate positive is paying attention to employees' emotional needs (Ozcelik et al. 2008), indicating the allowance of all emotions (Bar-tal et al. 2007). Thus, encouraging leadership (Maimone and Sinclair 2010) as well as active initiatives (Ozcelik et al. 2008) can be used to create positivity. This often necessitates high emotional intelligence (cf. Salovey and Mayer 1990; Goleman 1998; Mayer and Caruso 2002) from managers.

Positive emotions also stem from organizational identification (cf. Raitis et al. 2017). In maintaining identification over a change period, perceived continuity is essential (van Knippenberg et al. 2002). The attributes attached to *who we are* (e.g. Gioia et al. 2013; Raitis 2015) are central in building an emotional bond to the organization (cf. Huy 1999; Pratt 2000). Attachment, in turn, fuels positive organizational behaviour (Huy 1999). Nevertheless, to be able to change identity, unlearning must occur. This transition necessitates psychological safety, highlighting the importance of creating a positive vision of the future and offering employees engagement opportunities (Schein 1996).

While emotionally positive refers to what is goal-congruent and pleasing, and negative to that which is goal-incongruent and displeasing (e.g. Lazarus 1991), it is important to note that in organizations, this subjective level is only one aspect of positivity. Positive, as we have learned in this book, can reflect a compelling future vision, the mutual benefits that can be gained through unity, or finding continuity in the organizational identity. Therefore, even though positive undeniably refers to something affirmative and hedonically pleasing, on the organizational level, the experience of positivity does not refer solely to positive emotions. Instead, positivity stems from feelings of security and openness, which are created through managerial interest in employees' emotional needs.

Similarly, it must be emphasized that positive and negative are not mutually exclusive alternatives, but both can occur independently and at a high or low arousal level (cf. Watson and Tellegen 1985; Russell and Carroll 1999). This further emphasizes the necessity of understanding and detecting all emotions in order to create positivity. While alleviating worries alone cannot create positivity, the continued experience of the negative can hinder the emergence of the positive. Similarly, it is important to consider emotions at all activation levels (cf. Ashkanasy and Dorris 2017). Whereas highly activating emotions such as anger or excitement may be most visible, the less activating anxiety or calmness are no less important in terms of building positivity and shared understanding.

3 Implications and Limitations

3.1 Implications for Research

This book has outlined the meaning of positive change management following acquisitions, identifying five steps: detecting and understanding employee emotions, creating a sense of excitement and readiness, forming a compelling vision of the future, responding to employees' emotions and encouraging employees to identify with the new organization. While skilled managers can follow these steps unconsciously, planning post-acquisition change to include them will likely lead to more positive outcomes. It is particularly important to note that simply decreasing worries is not enough to create positivity regarding change. Instead, positive emotion triggers should actively be offered to the employees.

In building unity following acquisitions, this book has highlighted the crucial difference between positive emotions reflecting the pre- and post-acquisition organizations. In order to create readiness for change, positivity must be triggered regarding the post-acquisition company. If positivity only reflects the pre-acquisition company, employees are likely to resist integration. However, it is important to note that not all emotions regarding the pre-acquisition company are bad. If positivity is also felt towards the post-acquisition company, emotions reflecting the pre-acquisition organization do not necessarily eat away at the integrated company. Based on the findings, a positive emotional climate is particularly supportive for successful post-acquisition integration, as it enhances the positive behavioural outcomes of positive emotions. This necessitates a clear compelling vision to work towards.

In finding continuity, this book has emphasized how employee emotions reflect organizational identity and link with different change-related attitudes. Emphasizing the human factor in organizations, the process of post-acquisition change was identified as including an inherently emotional element. Often this emotional element is connected to the pre-acquisition organizational identity, stemming from the emotional bond employees have established with the company. Thus, even if change itself takes the company in a positive direction, it may be experienced as emotionally difficult. In this regard, change resistance is more a question of repelling the new attributes than of actively behaving in ways that undermine the change. Therefore, recognizing potential identity struggles, seeing the change all the way through, helping employees create shared meaning, highlighting what is enduring and allowing the employees time to mourn for perceived losses are essential in post-acquisition identity change.

In Chap. 1, this book identified several research gaps. First, this book has tackled the inconsistent and undertheorized nature of the discussion regarding emotions in the acquisition literature (cf. Reus 2012; Zagelmeyer et al. 2016). The key methods for achieving this aim are the clear and explicit definitions of concepts and their interrelations throughout this book. Figure 5.1 collects these together.

At the core of Fig. 5.1 are group emotions. These are the group-based and group-shared experiences (Menges and Kilduff 2015) that guide collective behaviour. At the heart of group emotions are the individual members of the group who have positive or negative experiences based on cognitive appraisal (e.g. Lazarus 1991). These emotions are also linked to those emerging in the emotional climate, where the climate is likely to induce similarly valenced emotions and outcomes (Bar-tal et al. 2007), again leading to collective behaviour. Affective events at work (e.g. Weiss and Cropanzano 1996) trigger emotions, which reflect the surrounding emotional climate. Affective events may also cause change resistance, for example when facing identity change (cf. van Knippenberg et al. 2002). Organizational identity refers to the collective sense of *who we are* (e.g. Raitis 2015), the central, distinctive and enduring attributes of the organization (Albert and Whetten 1985). Organizational identification occurs when individuals attach the same attributes to the self as to the organization (Ashforth and Mael 1989; Dutton et al. 1994). Emotional

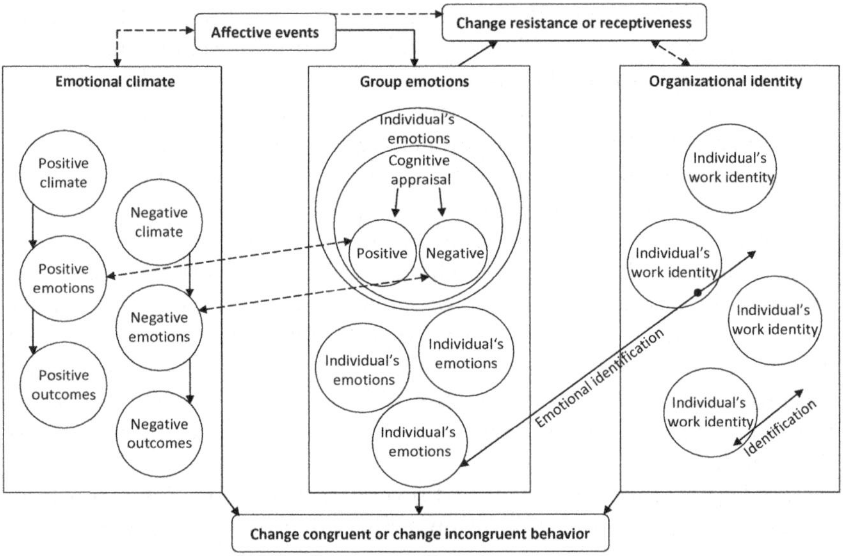

Fig. 5.1 The relationships between different emotional concepts

identification highlights the emotional bond experienced with the organization as well as the emotions that are born related to the organization (Raitis et al. 2017). Organizational identity also influences collective behaviour (van Knippenberg et al. 2002; Ashforth et al. 2020).

Second, this book has tackled the previous negative bias in the existing acquisition literature regarding emotions (Graebner et al. 2017). Through a focus on positive emotions, unity and continuity, this book has highlighted the many ways in which the literature and empirical evidence have shown increasing positivity following acquisitions. This is clearly connected to the third contribution that this book makes; the light shed on emotion management following acquisitions (cf. Huy 2012; Steigenberger 2015). Through exploring successful management in different emotional settings, this book has added depth to the discussion on managing emotions during change periods. Finally, this book has revealed some of the dynamics between individual and group emotions on the one hand, and group emotions and organizational outcomes on the other hand (cf. Ashkanasy et al. 2017; Parke and Seo 2017), thus helping scholars connect the dots between the different levels at which emotions emerge, and the collective outcomes they trigger.

One of the underlying objectives of this book has been to introduce scholars to different types of emotion-focused case studies conducted in the acquisition context. Through these illustrative case examples, this book encourages other scholars to adopt mixed and qualitative designs to conduct rigorous fieldwork. Because emotion is a highly subjective topic and the acquisition context can be idiosyncratic, including qualitative designs can highly advance our understanding of the dynamic, complex and intricate nature of successful emotion management following acquisitions.

3.2 Implications for Practice

Emotional skills in the workplace have gained increasing attention in the mainstream media. For example, *The 2018 Future of Jobs Report* published by the World Economic Forum (WEF 2018) indicates that by 2022, emotional intelligence will be among the key skills of employees entering the work force. The *Harvard Business Review* encourages companies to focus on the softer side of performance (Ignatius 2016) and find ways for coping with stress (Zhang et al. 2019), increasing self-compassion at work (Chen 2018), as well as cultivating courage (Detert 2018). Similarly,

Forbes discusses how mental strength can help deal with emotions (Morin 2020), how emotional contagion can be used strategically (Warrell 2020), how leaders can benefit from emotion regulation at work (Pollack 2020) and how team emotions can be managed (Inam 2020). This undeniable attention given to emotions signals the practical importance of the topic.

The insight from this book gives managers the opportunity to understand employee emotions following change much better, thus allowing improved planning in terms of human reactions. While this book centres on post-acquisition change, it is very likely that similar reactions also emerge following other types of organizational change. Thus, this book enables better planning and analysis of change efforts, highlighting ways to ease the process. At the same time, this book highlights the dynamic nature of employee reactions to change, indicating that some flexibility is often necessary in order to reach the best outcomes.

One of the key messages of this book is that employees may experience change as major, even if top management considers the change to be minute. This is due to the emotional attachment employees often have to the status quo. Thus, when the accustomed norms and practices are perceived as threatened, protectionist attitudes arise. Finding and emphasizing the continuity of the positive triggers that correspond with the employees' emotional attachment, such as company values or identity, can greatly ease change efforts. Particularly a clear positive vision of the future of the company can help engage employees in change efforts. Another key message of the book is engagement. Employees are likely to become more proactive towards change when they perceive that they have ownership of the change process. Thus, engaging employees in the change, for example through socialization efforts, or inviting them to take part in the planning, can greatly enhance their motivation to change. Particularly following acquisitions, this often centres on building a sense of unity between the acquisition partners through finding what is similar and mutually beneficial. Table 5.2 presents the collected managerial implications of this book.

This book suggests that anticipating emotions and their triggers following acquisitions can help practitioners pre-attune to emotion management. This is important particularly due to the tendency of employees to react emotionally regardless of the objective extent of the change. In order to ensure the skills necessary for emotion management, emotional intelligence and an interest in positive change efforts are beneficial. Nevertheless, emotional leadership is a strenuous activity, meaning that even the best managers need support in carrying out the change process.

Table 5.2 Managerial implications

Theme	*Desirable actions*
Managers	• Anticipate potential emotion triggers and resulting employee emotions • Ensure integration management possesses emotional intelligence and emotional leadership skills • Ensure that managers are supported in their efforts
Employee emotions	• Detect and understand employee emotions • Consider the individual, group, pre-acquisition and post-acquisition organizational levels in anticipating emotion triggers • Emphasize positive emotion triggers and alleviate worries • Create positivity towards the post-acquisition organization
Emotional climate	• Emphasize positive elements in the emotional climate • Form a compelling vision of the future • Create a sense of excitement and readiness • Allow employees to experience and express all kinds of emotions
Identity	• Detect and ensure the continuity of key attributes • Help create shared meaning • Allow time for identity transition • Strengthen the achieved integration through encouraging employees to identify with the new organization

In generating positive change, it is crucial to be able to detect and understand employee emotions. The realization that emotions are human, and therefore not inherently bad or harmful, is essential in being able to manage collective emotions. Similarly, it is beneficial to recognize that emotions occur and thus are contagious between different organizational levels. Emphasizing what employees perceive as positive and alleviating what is experienced as negative helps ease the change process. Furthermore, highlighting what is positive regarding the post-acquisition company may be particularly influential in building unity.

Emphasizing what the employees already perceive as positive can help maintain a positive climate following change. Nevertheless, this positivity will start to deteriorate if the employees cannot detect a compelling vision of the future to work towards. Thus, creating a sense of excitement and readiness through emphasizing the positive aspects of integration is beneficial. Even so, for employees to experience psychological safety at work, it is important that all emotions are allowed and accepted. Thus, helping employees cope with their emotions is a key step in maintaining a positive climate.

Continuity is equally, if not even more importantly, a part of identity transitions during change. Identifying the key aspects of what is central, distinctive and enduring in the organization can help draw a parallel between the old and the new, and thereby ease employee identification with the new organization. Using pre-designed socialization efforts to engage employees in creating shared meaning can ease the process greatly. Nevertheless, if extensive identity change is imminent, enough time should be allotted for this often lengthy process.

3.3 Limitations and Suggestions for Future Research

As in many case studies, some key limitations in this book are connected to the data. Although suitable for the purpose of this book, the data does not allow for strong arguments on the generalizability of the findings. Thus, future research with more cases or an alternative methodology is necessary to add weight to the ideas presented here. In addition, the POS lens may have placed a positive bias on this book. Thus, future research could benefit from a closer look at how negative emotions emerge during and influence positive change management. Similarly, this book has discussed three friendly acquisition case contexts. It is likely that research on hostile acquisitions will reveal novel insights. Finally, this book reveals the potential benefits of positive change management, but it would be interesting for future research to look at how companies could build positive change capability (cf. Andreeva and Ritala 2016), which highlights the continuous and dynamic nature of change.

References

Albert, S., & Whetten, D. A. (1985). Organizational identity. *Research in Organizational Behavior, 7*, 263–295.

Andreeva, T., & Ritala, P. (2016). What are the sources of capability dynamism? Reconceptualizing dynamic capabilities from the perspective of organizational change. *Baltic Journal of Management, 11*(3), 238–259. https://doi.org/10.1108/BJM-02-2015-0049.

Ashforth, B. E., & Mael, F. (1989). Social identity theory and the organization. *The Academy of Management Review, 14*(1), 20–39. https://doi.org/10.2307/258189.

Ashforth, B. E., Schinoff, B. S., & Brickson, S. L. (2020). "My company is friendly," "mine's a rebel": Anthropomorphism and shifting organizational identity from "what" to "who". *Academy of Management Review, 45*(1), 29–57. https://doi.org/10.5465/amr.2016.0496.

Ashkanasy, N. M. (2003). Emotions in organizations: A multi-level perspective. *Research in Multi-Level Issues, 2*, 9–54. https://doi.org/10.1016/S1475-9144(03)02002-2.

Ashkanasy, N. M., & Dorris, A. D. (2017). Emotions in the workplace. *Annual Review of Organizational Psychology and Organizational Behavior, 4*, 67–90.

Ashkanasy, N. M., Humphrey, R. H., & Huy, Q. N. (2017). Integrating emotions and affect in theories of management. *Academy of Management Review, 42*(2), 175–189.

Avey, J. B., Wernsing, T. S., & Luthans, F. (2008). Can positive employees help positive organizational change? Impact of psychological capital and emotions on relevant attitudes and behaviors. *Journal of Applied Behavioral Science, 44*(1), 48–70. https://doi.org/10.1177/0021886307311470.

Bar-tal, D., Halperin, E., & DeRivera, J. (2007). Collective emotions in conflict situations: Societal implications. *Journal of Societal Issues, 63*(2), 441–460.

Birkinshaw, J., Bresman, H., & Håkanson, L. (2000). Managing the post-acquisition integration process: How the human integration and task integration processes interact to foster value creation. *Journal of Management Studies, 37*(3), 395–425. https://doi.org/10.1111/1467-6486.00186.

Cameron, K. (2008). Paradox in positive organizational change. *Journal of Applied Behavioral Science, 44*(1), 7–24. https://doi.org/10.1177/0021886308314703.

Cameron, K. (2012). *Positive leadership: Strategies for extraordinary performance* (2nd ed.). San Francisco, CA: Berrett-Koehler.

Cameron, K., Dutton, J., & Quinn, R. (2003). Foundations of positive organizational scholarship. In K. Cameron, J. Dutton, & R. Quinn (Eds.), *Positive organizational scholarship: Foundations of a new discipline* (pp. 3–13). San Francisco, CA: Berrett-Koehler.

Cartwright, S., & Cooper, C. L. (1993). The role of culture compatibility in successful organizational marriage. *Academy of Management Perspectives, 7*(2), 57–70. https://doi.org/10.5465/AME.1993.9411302324.

Chen, S. (2018). Give yourself a break: The power of self-compassion. *Harvard Business Review, 96*(5), 116–123.

Detert, J. (2018). Cultivating everyday courage. *Harvard Business Review, 96*(6), 128–135.

Dutton, J. E., Dukerich, J. M., & Harquail, C. V. (1994). Organizational images and member identification. *Administrative Science Quarterly, 39*(2), 239–263. https://doi.org/10.3233/CBM-130327.

Fischer, A. H., & Manstead, A. S. R. (2008). Social functions of emotion. In M. Lewis, J. Haviland-Jones, & L. F. Barrett (Eds.), *Handbook of emotions* (3rd ed., pp. 456–468). New York: The Guilford Press.

Fredrickson, B. L. (2001). The role of positive emotions in positive psychology. *American Psychologist, 56*(3), 218–226. https://doi.org/10.1037/0003-066X.56.3.218.

Gioia, D. A., Patvardhan, S. D., Hamilton, A. L., & Corley, K. G. (2013). Organizational identity formation and change. *Academy of Management Annals, 7*(1), 123–193. https://doi.org/10.1080/19416520.2013.762225.
Goldenberg, A., Saguy, T., & Halperin, E. (2014). How group-based emotions are shaped by collective emotions: Evidence for emotional transfer and emotional burden. *Journal of Personality and Social Psychology, 107*(4), 581–596. https://doi.org/10.1037/a0037462.
Goleman, D. (1998). What makes a leader. *Harvard Business Review, 76*(6), 93–102. https://doi.org/10.13445/j.cnki.t.e.r.2014.03.007.
Graebner, M. E., Heimeriks, K. H., Huy, Q. N., & Vaara, E. (2017). The process of postmerger integration: A review and agenda for future research. *Academy of Management Annals, 11*(1), 1–32. https://doi.org/10.5465/annals.2014.0078.
Huy, Q. N. (1999). Emotional capability, emotional intelligence, and radical change. *Academy of Management Review, 24*(2), 325–345. https://doi.org/10.5465/AMR.1999.1893939.
Huy, Q. N. (2012). Emotions in strategic organization: Opportunities for impactful research. *Strategic Organization, 10*(3), 240–247. https://doi.org/10.1177/1476127012453107.
Ignatius, A. (2016). From the editor. *Harvard Business Review, 94*, 1), 1.
Inam, H. (2020). Three tools to manage emotions in your team. *Forbes*, Retrieved June 18, from https://www.forbes.com/sites/hennainam/2020/06/18/
Kemper, T. D. (2002). Predicting emotions in groups: Some lessons from September 11. *The Sociological Review, 50*(S2), 53–68.
Kiefer, T. (2005). Feeling bad: Antecedents and consequences of negative emotions in ongoing change. *Journal of Organizational Behavior, 26*(8), 875–897.
Larsson, R., & Lubatkin, M. (2001). Achieving acculturation in mergers and acquisitions: An international case survey. *Human Relations, 54*(12), 1573–1607. https://doi.org/10.1177/00187267015412002.
Lazarus, R. (1991). *Emotion and adaptation*. New York: Oxford University Press.
Maimone, F., & Sinclair, M. (2010). Affective climate, organizational creativity, and knowledge creation: Case study of an automotive company. In W. Zerbe, C. Härtel, & N. Ashkanasy (Eds.), *Emotions and organizational dynamism: Research on emotion in organizations* (Vol. 6, pp. 309–332). Bingley: Emerald. https://doi.org/10.1108/S1746-9791(2010)0000006016.
Mayer, J., & Caruso, D. (2002). The effective leader: Understanding and applying emotional intelligence. *Ivey Business Journal, 67*(2), 1–5.
Menges, J. I., & Kilduff, M. (2015). Group emotions: Cutting the gordian knots concerning terms, levels of analysis, and processes. *Academy of Management Annals, 9*(1), 845–928. https://doi.org/10.1080/19416520.2015.1033148.
Morin, A. (2020). How mentally strong people deal with uncomfortable emotions. *Forbes*, Retrieved May 18, from https://www.forbes.com/sites/amymorin/2020/05/18/h

Oreg, S., Bartunek, J. M., Lee, G., & Do, B. (2018). An affect-based model of recipients' responses to organizational change events. *Academy of Management Review, 43*(1), 65–86. https://doi.org/10.5465/amr.2014.0335.

Ozcelik, H., Langton, N., & Aldrich, H. (2008). Doing well and doing good: The relationship between leadership practices. *Journal of Managerial Psychology, 23*(2), 186–203. https://doi.org/10.1108/02683940810850817.

Parke, M. R., & Seo, M.-G. (2017). The role of affect climate in organizational effectiveness. *Academy of Management Review, 42*(2), 334–360.

Pollack, J. (2020). 4 ways leaders can regulate their emotions at work. *Forbes*, Retrieved June 30, from https://www.forbes.com/sites/jeremypollack/2020/06

Pratt, M. G. (2000). The good the bad and the ambivalent: Managing identification among Amway distributors. *Administrative Science Quarterly, 45*(3), 456–493.

Raitis, J. (2015). *Identity and multinational corporations: Building unity within diversity*. Turku: University of Turku.

Raitis, J., Harikkala-Laihinen, R., Hassett, M., & Nummela, N. (2017). Finding positivity during a major organizational change: In search of triggers of employees' positive perceptions and feelings. In W. Zerbe, C. Härtel, N. Ashkanasy, & L. Petitta (Eds.), *Emotions and identity: Research on emotion in organizations* (Vol. 13, pp. 3–16). https://doi.org/10.1108/S1746-979120170000013001.

Reus, T. H. (2012). Culture's consequences for emotional attending during cross-border acquisition implementation. *Journal of World Business, 47*(3), 342–351. https://doi.org/10.1016/j.jwb.2011.05.002.

Roberts, L. M. (2006). Shifting the lens on organizational life: The added value of positive scholarship. *Academy of Management Review, 31*(2), 292–305.

Russell, J. A., & Carroll, J. M. (1999). On the bipolarity of positive and negative affect. *Psychological Bulletin, 125*(1), 3–30. https://doi.org/10.1037/0033-2909.125.1.3.

Salovey, P., & Mayer, J. D. (1990). Emotional intelligence and its relationship to other intelligences. *Cognition and Personality, 9*(3), 185–211. https://doi.org/10.1037/0022-3514.50.2.421.

Schein, E. H. (1996). Kurt Lewin's change theory in the field and in the classroom: Notes toward a model of managed learning. *Systems Practice, 9*(1), 27–47. https://doi.org/10.1007/BF02173417.

Steigenberger, N. (2015). Emotions in sensemaking: A change management perspective. *Journal of Organizational Change Management, 28*(3), 432–451. https://doi.org/10.1108/JOCM-05-2014-0095.

Teerikangas, S. (2012). Dynamics of acquired firm pre-acquisition employee reactions. *Journal of Management, 38*(2), 599–639. https://doi.org/10.1177/0149206310383908.

van Knippenberg, D., van Knippenberg, B., Monden, L., & de Lima, F. (2002). Organizational identification after a merger: A social identity perspective. *British Journal of Social Psychology, 41*(2), 233–252. https://doi.org/10.1348/014466602760060228.

Warrell, M. (2020). Emotional contagion is potent: Use it to spread possibility, not pessimism. *Forbes*, Retrieved May 6, from https://www.forbes.com/sites/margiewarrell/2020/05.

Watson, D., & Tellegen, A. (1985). Toward a consensual structure of mood. *Psychological Bulletin, 98*(2), 219–235. https://doi.org/10.1037/0033-2909.98.2.219.

Weiss, H., & Cropanzano, R. (1996). Affective events theory: A theoretical discussion of the structure, causes and consequences of affective experiences at work. In B. M. Staw & L. Cummings (Eds.), *Research in organizational behavior: An annual series of analytical essays and critical reviews* (pp. 1–74). US: JAI Press and Elsevier Science.

World Economic Forum. (2018). The future of jobs report. Retrieved July 5, 2020, from http://www3.weforum.org/docs/WEF_Future_of_Jobs_2018.pdf

Zagelmeyer, S., Sinkovics, R. R., Sinkovics, N., & Kusstatscher, V. (2016). Exploring the link between management communication and emotions in mergers and acquisitions. *Canadian Journal of Administrative Sciences, 35*(1), 93–106.

Zhang, C., Myers, C. G., & Mayer, D. M. (2019). To cope with stress, try learning something new. *Harvard Business Review, 97*(Special Issue), 31–33.

Index

R. Harikkala-Laihinen, *Managing Emotions in Organizations*,
https://doi.org/10.1007/978-3-030-60567-4

The manufacturer's authorised representative in the EU is Springer Nature Customer Service Centre GmbH, Europaplatz 3, 69115 Heidelberg, Germany. If you have any concerns regarding our products, please contact ProductSafety@springernature.com

Printed and bound by CPI Group (UK) Ltd, Croydon, CR0 4YY
30/09/2026
02225470-0002